ANSYS® Tutorial

Release 11.0

Structural & Thermal Analysis Using the ANSYS Release 11.0 Environment

Kent L. Lawrence

Mechanical and Aerospace Engineering
University of Texas at Arlington

ISBN: 978-1-58503-400-0

SDC
PUBLICATIONS

Schroff Development Corporation

www.schroff.com
www.schroff-europe.com

Kent L. Lawrence is Professor of Mechanical and Aerospace Engineering, University of Texas at Arlington where he has served as Graduate Advisor, Chair of the Department, and has supervised the graduate work of over one hundred masters and PhD students. He is an ASME Fellow, author of *ANSYS Workbench Tutorial*, SDC Publications, 2006 and coauthor with Robert L. Woods of the text *Modeling and Simulation of Dynamic Systems*, Prentice-Hall, 1997.

ISBN: 978-1-58503-400-0

Dedicated to

Ben, Annie, Jamison, Mary Claire, and Kent III, potential twenty-first century engineers, one and all.

TABLE OF CONTENTS

LESSON 3 – AXISYMMETRIC PROBLEMS

LESSON 4 – THREE-DIMENSIONAL PROBLEMS

LESSON 8 – p-METHOD

LESSON 9 – SELECTED TOPICS

INDEX

PREFACE

The nine lessons in the ANSYS Tutorial introduce the reader to effective engineering problem solving through the use of this powerful finite element analysis tool. Topics include trusses, plane stress, plane strain, axisymmetric problems, 3-D problems, beams, plates, conduction/convection heat transfer, thermal stress, and p-method solutions. It is designed for practicing and student engineers alike and is suitable for use with an organized course of instruction or for self-study.

The ANSYS software (such as ANSYS Mechanical, ANSYS Academic Teaching, ANSYS Academic Research, etc) is one of the most mature, widely distributed and popular commercial FEM (Finite Element Method) programs available. In continuous use and refinement since 1970, its long history of development has resulted in a code with a vast range of capabilities. This tutorial introduces a basic set of those to the reader. An extensive on-line help system, a number of excellent tutorial web sites, and other printed resources are available for further study.

Several years ago I started using the Pro/ENGINEER Tutorial by Prof. Roger Toogood in a university course containing equal parts parametric, feature-based solid modeling and finite element analysis. The tutorial approach worked so well for the solid modeling that it became the inspiration for this FEM book.

I am most appreciative of the long-time support of research and teaching efforts in our universities provided by ANSYS, Inc and for the assistance in the preparation of this book provided by Paul Lethbridge of ANSYS.

Heartfelt thanks also go to Mr. Opart Gomonwattanapanich and Mr. Mukund Narasimhan who read portions of the material herein as well as test-solved a number of the problems. I also appreciate the comments and suggestions provided by Prof. Wen Chan and by Dr. C. Y. Lin.

Stephen Schroff of SDC Publications urged me to try the Toogood book and has been very helpful to my efforts in the preparation of this material. To Stephen I am most indebted as well as to Ms. Mary Schmidt for her careful assistance with the manuscript.

Special thanks go as usual to Carol Lawrence, ever supportive and always willing to proof even the most arcane and cryptic stuff.

Please feel free to point out any problems that you may notice with the tutorials in this book. Your comments are welcome at **lawrence@mae.uta.edu** and can only help to improve what is presented here. Additions and corrections to the book are posted on **mae.uta.edu/~lawrence/ANSYStutorial**, so check here for errata to the version that you are using.

Kent L. Lawrence

NOTES:

Introduction

I-1 OVERVIEW

Engineers routinely use the **Finite Element Method (FEM)** to solve everyday problems of **stress**, **deformation**, **heat transfer**, **fluid flow**, **electromagnetics**, etc. using commercial as well as special purpose computer codes. This book presents a collection of tutorial lessons for **ANSYS**, one of the most versatile and widely used of the commercial finite element programs.

The lessons discuss linear static response for problems involving truss, plane stress, plane strain, axisymmetric, solid, beam, and plate structural elements. Example problems in heat transfer, thermal stress, mesh creation and transferring models from CAD solid modelers to ANSYS are also included.

The tutorials progress from simple to complex. Each lesson can be mastered in a short period of time, and Lessons 1 through 7 should all be completed to obtain a thorough understanding of basic ANSYS structural analysis. ANSYS running on Windows2000 was used in the preparation of this text.

I-2 THE FEM PROCESS

The finite element process is generally divided into three distinct phases

1. **PREPROCESSING** – Build the FEM model.

2. **SOLVING** – Solve the equations.

3. **POSTPROCESSING** – Display and evaluate the results.

The execution of the three steps may be done through a **batch** process, an **interactive** session, or a **combination** of batch and interactive processes. These tutorials cover all three approaches.

I-3 THE LESSONS

A short description of each of the ANSYS Tutorial lessons follows.

Lesson 1 utilizes simple, two-dimensional **truss** models to introduce basic ANSYS concepts and operation principles.

Lesson 2 covers problems in **plane stress** and **plane strain** including a discussion of determining stress concentration effects. Geometry from a CAD solid modeler is imported into ANSYS for FEM analysis.

Lesson 3 discusses the solution of **axisymmetric** problems wherein geometry, material properties, loadings and boundary conditions are rotationally symmetric with respect to a central axis.

Lesson 4 introduces three-dimensional **tetrahedron** and **brick** element modeling and the various options available for the analysis of complex geometries. Importing models from CAD systems is also discussed.

Lesson 5 treats problems in structural analysis where the most suitable modeling choice is a **beam** element. Both two-dimensional and three-dimensional examples are presented.

Lesson 6 covers the use of **shell** (plate) elements for modeling of structural problems of various types.

Lesson 7 presents tutorials in the solution of conduction/convection problems of **heat transfer** in solids. It concludes with an analysis of a case of **thermal stress** in an object whose temperature distribution has been determined by an ANSYS thermal analysis.

Lesson 8 introduces the **p-method** of finite element analysis wherein the accuracy of elements used in the solution is adjusted in order to give results which meet preset convergence requirements.

Lesson 9 covers additional short topics of interest to the ANSYS user. These include problems with multiple load cases, determining natural frequencies of structural systems, and others.

The lessons are necessarily of varying length and can be worked through from start to finish. Those with previous ANSYS experience may want to skip around a bit as needs and interests dictate.

I-4 THE *ANSYS* INTERFACE

To start ANSYS on a Windows-based system, select **ANSYS** or **ANSYS Product Launcher** from the desktop menu shown below.

Figure I-1 ANSYS desktop menu.

The **Product Launcher** provides an opportunity to select a number of system options including the default working directory. This is very helpful in some network startup situations.

Figure I-2 ANSYS Product Launcher.

Figure I-3 shows the **ANSYS interface** with **Utility Menu** across the top followed by the ANSYS **Command Input** area, **Main Menu**, **Graphics** display, and ANSYS **Toolbar**.

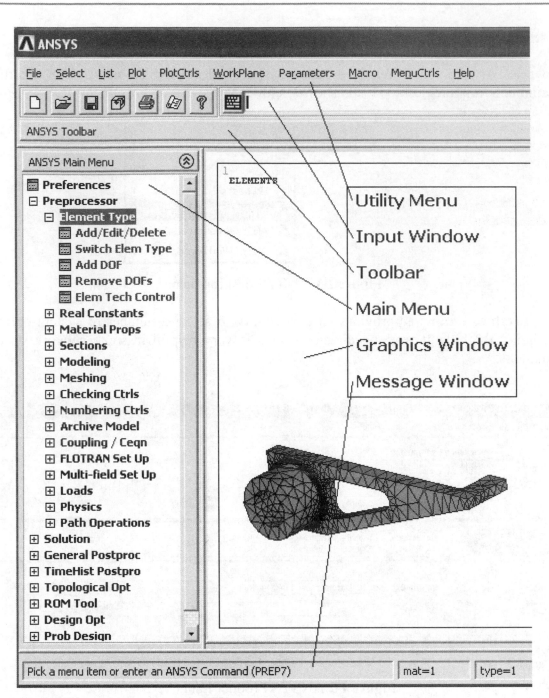

Figure I-3 ANSYS Interface.

Be sure to check the **Message Window** for prompts if you need to know what is the next action you should take to complete an operation.

Program actions can be initiated in a number of ways; by **text file input**, by **command inputs**, or by **menu picks**. In some cases (creating lists of quantities, for example) there may be more than one menu pick sequence that produces the same results. These ideas are explored in the lessons that follow.

I-5 SUMMARY

The tutorials in this book explain some of the many engineering problem solution options available in ANSYS. It is important to remember that while practically anyone can learn which buttons to push to make the program work, the user must first posses an adequate engineering background, then give careful consideration to the assumptions inherent in the modeling process and finally give an equally careful evaluation of the computed results.

In short, model building and output evaluation based upon sound fundamental principles of engineering and physics is the key to using any program such as ANSYS correctly.

NOTES:

Lesson 1

Trusses

1-1 OVERVIEW

Simple truss structural analysis is used in this lesson to introduce the FEA framework and the general concepts that will be used in the lessons that follow. Truss modeling may not be your primary goal in undertaking these lessons, but it provides us a convenient vehicle for beginning a study of finite element methods with ANSYS. The three tutorials explore:

♦ Creating a text file FEM model definition.

♦ Problem solving interactively using the ANSYS interface.

♦ Combining text file input and interactive solution methods.

In addition, a number of additional truss modeling possibilities and formulations are demonstrated.

1-2 INTRODUCTION

Some structures are built from elements connected by pins at their joints. These **two force elements** can carry only axial tensile or compressive forces and stresses.

Figure 1-1 Two-force element.

Other structures built of long slender members that are welded or bolted together may carry such small bending and torsion loads that they can be accurately analyzed by using a pin-jointed model.

ANSYS provides a comprehensive library of elements for use in the development of models of physical systems. While engineering problems always arise from consideration of some real-life 3D situation, 2D models are often times sufficient for describing the behavior and therefore widely used. The ANSYS two-force element **LINK1** is used for planar (2D) truss models.

1-3 SHELF TRUSS

Figure 1-2 shows a steel shelf we wish to analyze to determine the **maximum stress** and **deflection** of the support structure. To do this, we consider a two-dimensional model of the pin-jointed structure that supports each end of the shelf.

Figure 1-2 Shelf.

Depending on the connection details, there could be some twisting of the horizontal truss element of our problem. Twisting is ignored here but can be considered in a more detailed model later if necessary. Good engineering practice often involves first analyzing the simplest model that can address the major questions being considered and subsequently developing more complex models as understanding of the problem grows. Figure 1-3 displays the FEM model of the shelf support.

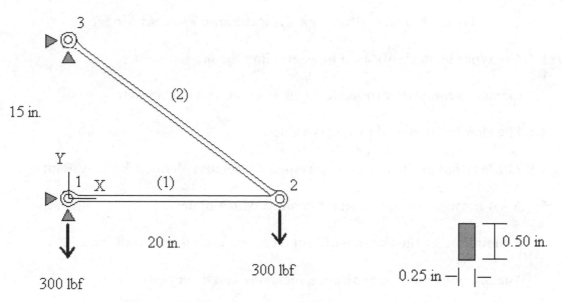

Figure 1-3 Simple truss and element cross section.

The XYZ coordinate system is the **global axis** for the problem. The location and orientation of this reference axis system is selected by the engineer in setting up the model. **Nodes 1, 2,** and **3** are points where **elements (1)** and **(2)** join each other and/or the support structure. Elements (1) and (2) carry only axial loads, and ANSYS link1 type elements are used to model their behavior.

The small triangles are used to indicate a displacement constraint, no motion in this case. We assume a uniform distribution of the 1200 lbf shelf load to its four supports. The 300 lbf force at node 1 is reacted directly by the support at that node but is shown anyway for completeness.

The **area** of the structural elements is 0.25 x 0.50 = **0.125 in²**, and the values of the material properties we will use for steel are: **elastic modulus, E = 30 x 10⁶ psi**; **Poisson's ratio,** $\nu = 0.27$.

A free body at node 2 shows that element (1) will be in **compression** and element (2) will be in **tension**. We can use this observation to check the computed results.

Figure 1-4 Free body of node 2.

We can now list the seven input quantities that are needed to characterize a typical finite element model. These items are defined during the **Preprocessing** phase.

Items that Constitute of a Typical Finite Element Model

1. The types of elements used in assembling the model.

2. Element geometric properties such as areas, thicknesses, etc.

3. The element material property values.

4. The location of the nodes with respect to the user defined XYZ system.

5. A list showing which elements connect which nodes.

6. A definition of the nodes with displacement boundary conditions.

7. The loadings, their magnitudes, locations and directions.

In the tutorial below we define the model for this problem by creating a text file that contains the seven groups listed above. The Preprocessing step is then performed when ANSYS reads the text file. The Solution and Post Processing steps are performed interactively.

1-4 TUTORIAL 1A – SHELF TRUSS

Follow the steps below to analyze the truss model. The tutorial is divided into separate Preprocessing, Solution, and Postprocessing steps.

Objective: Determine the maximum stress and deflection. Check for buckling.

PREPROCESSING

1. Create Input Data File - Use a text editor such as Notepad to prepare a file that contains the information shown below. Lines beginning with '**/**' contain **ANSYS operations** to be performed. Other lines contain **input data** or comments. A **comment** begins with '**!**'.

Save the file as **T1A.txt** or another convenient name. To obtain meaningful and easily interpreted results, we use a consistent set of units for all input quantities, **inches** and **pounds force** in this case.

Add your name to the title 'Simple Truss' to identify the plotted output.

```
/FILNAM,Tutorial-1A
/title, Simple Truss
/prep7

et, 1, link1                 ! Element type no.1 is LINK1

mp, ex, 1, 3.e7              ! Material Properties: E for material no. 1
mp, prxy, 1, 0.27           ! & poisson's ratio for material no.1

r, 1, 0.125                 ! Real Constant number 1 is 0.125
                            ! (Cross sectional area)

n, 1,  0.0,  0.0, 0.0       ! Node 1 is located at ( 0.0, 0.0, 0.0)
n, 2, 20.0,  0.0, 0.0
n, 3,  0.0, 15.0, 0.0

en, 1, 1, 2                 ! Element Number 1 connects nodes 1 & 2
en, 2, 2, 3

d, 1, ux, 0.                ! Displacement at node 1 in x-dir is zero
d, 1, uy, 0.                ! Displacement at node 1 in y-dir is zero
d, 3, ux, 0.
d, 3, uy, 0.

f, 1, fy, -300.             ! Force at node 1 in y-direction is -300.
f, 2, fy, -300.             ! Force at node 2 in y-direction is -300.
```

2. To start **ANSYS Select ANSYS** or **ANSYS Product Launcher > Run** from the menu below. (For more on **Product Launcher** options, see the previous chapter, **Introduction**.)

Figure 1-5 Desktop menu.

The ANSYS interface shown below includes the **Utility Menu** across the top followed by the ANSYS **Command Input** area, the **Main Menu**, the **Graphics** display, and the ANSYS **Toolbar**. The **ANSYS interface** is shown in the figure below.

The **Jobname** and **Title** to be used for this analysis are contained in the first two lines of the text file. ANSYS will use the file name for any files created or saved during this computation.

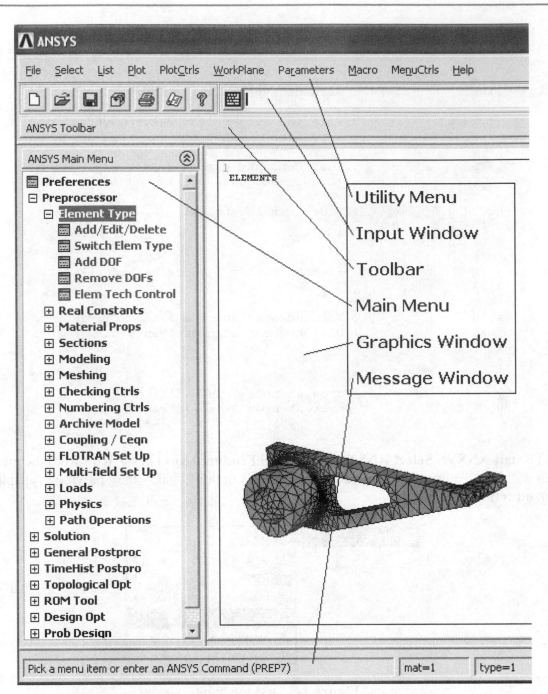

Figure 1-6 ANSYS interface components.

In the tutorials in this book we will make extensive use of the Utility Menu, Main Menu and Graphics Window. It is easy to overlook the **message window** at the bottom left corner of the screen. When in doubt as to what to do next, check here first.

Set the working directory you want to use for this analysis.

3. Utility Menu > File > Change Directory

Figure 1-7 Set the working directory.

(If you want to use a different Jobname and/or a different title, use **Utility Menu >. File > Change Jobname ...** and **Utility Menu > File > Change Title ...**)

Next we will read the text data file you prepared for this problem into ANSYS.

4. Utility Menu > File > Read Input From   (Find and select the file **T1A.txt** that you prepared earlier.)

After the file is read, we will **display the model graphically** and check to see that the model is correctly defined.

Figure 1-8 File menu.

Graphical image manipulation can be performed using the Pan, Zoom, Rotate pull-down menu or the equivalent icons on the right border of the graphics screen. (**Utility Menu > PlotCtrls > Pan, Zoom, Rotate …**)

Figure 1-9 Pan, Zoom, Rotate menu and equivalent on-screen icons.

Turn on node and element numbering graphics options.

5. Utility Menu > PlotCtrls > Numbering > Node numbers ON, Element / Attrib numbers > Element numbers > OK

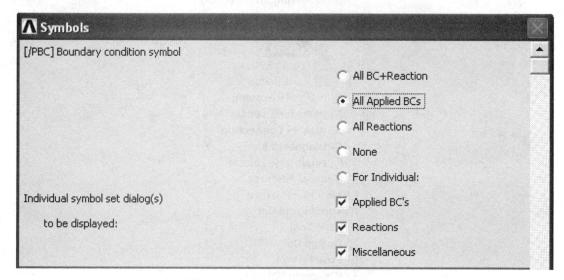

Figure 1-10 Numbering controls.

Setup the graphics to display boundary conditions and loads.

6. Utility Menu > PlotCtrls > Symbols > All Applied B.C.'s > OK

Figure 1-11 Symbols options.

(You may have to reset or adjust these plotting options from time to time during the analysis to obtain the graphic information you want to see.)

7. Fit **> Plot > Elements** (use Fit or Zoom, Pan controls as needed.)

The plot of your model is now displayed as shown in the figure to the right.

Figure 1-12 Plot of model.

SOLUTION

8. Main Menu > Solution > Solve > Current LS > OK

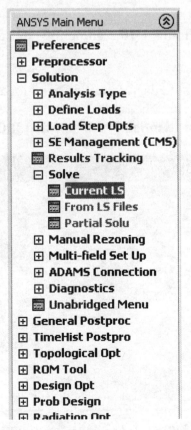

Figure 1-13 Solution menu.

The **/STATUS Command** window displays the problem parameters and the **Solve Current Load Step** window is shown. Check the solution options in the /STATUS window and if all is OK, in the **Solve Current Load Step** window, select **OK** to compute the solution.

```
/STATUS Command
File

                    L O A D   S T E P   O P T I O N S

    LOAD STEP NUMBER. . . . . . . . . . . . . . . .     2
    TIME AT END OF THE LOAD STEP. . . . . . . . . .   2.0000
    NUMBER OF SUBSTEPS. . . . . . . . . . . . . . .     1
    STEP CHANGE BOUNDARY CONDITIONS . . . . . . . .    NO
    PRINT OUTPUT CONTROLS . . . . . . . . . . . . .NO PRINTOUT
    DATABASE OUTPUT CONTROLS. . . . . . . . . . . .ALL DATA WRITTEN
                                                  FOR THE LAST SUBSTEP
```

Figure 1-14 Solution options.

```
Solve Current Load Step                          [X]

[SOLVE] Begin Solution of Current Load Step

Review the summary information in the lister window (entitled "/STATUS
Command"), then press OK to start the solution.


            [   OK   ]    [  Cancel  ]    [  Help  ]
```

Figure 1-15 Solve.

```
Note                                             [X]

   (i)    Solution is done!



                   [  Close  ]
```

Figure 1-16 Solution completion.

Once the solution is complete, **Close** the **Note** and **STATUS** windows. The **Raise Hidden** button near the top of the screen can be used to bring the STATUS window (or any other hidden window) to the foreground.

POSTPROCESSING

We can now **plot the results** of this analysis and also **list the computed values**.

9. Main Menu > General Postproc > Plot Results > Deformed Shape > Def. + Undef. > OK

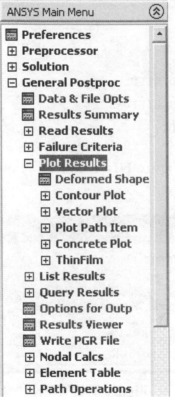

Figure 1-17 Postprocessing options.

Figure 1-18 Plot deformed shape options.

The following graphic is created.

Figure 1-19 Deformed shape plot.

Use **PlotCtrls > Hard Copy > To Printer** to print graphics. (**PlotCtrls > Style > Background,** uncheck **Display Picture Background** if need be.)

It is often very useful to **animate** the deflected shape to visualize how the structure is behaving. Make the following selections from the utility menu to create an animation.

10. Utility Menu > PlotCtrls > Animate > Deformed Shape > OK

Use the Raise Hidden button and Animation Controller to stop animation. A list of the computed results can be obtained from the **General Postprocessor Menu**.

Figure 1-20 Animation Controller.

11. Main Menu > General Postproc > List Results > Nodal Solution > DOF Solution > Displacement vector sum > OK

```
PRINT U    NODAL SOLUTION PER NODE

 ***** POST1 NODAL DEGREE OF FREEDOM LISTING *****

 LOAD STEP=     1  SUBSTEP=       1
  TIME=    1.0000      LOAD CASE=   0

 THE FOLLOWING DEGREE OF FREEDOM RESULTS ARE IN GLOBAL COORDINATES

    NODE      UX           UY           UZ           USUM
      1    0.0000        0.0000       0.0000        0.0000
      2  -0.21333E-02-0.84000E-02    0.0000        0.86667E-02
      3    0.0000        0.0000       0.0000        0.0000

 MAXIMUM ABSOLUTE VALUES
 NODE          2            2            0            2
 VALUE  -0.21333E-02-0.84000E-02    0.0000        0.86667E-02
```

Node 2 is the only node allowed to move in this simple model, and from the above we see that the **maximum deflections** are 0.0021 and 0.0084 inches to **left** and **down**. Although no design specifications were mentioned in the problem definition, the shelf support structure seems to be pretty stiff.

Let's check the stresses.

12. Main Menu > General Postproc > List Results > Element Solution > Line Element Results > Element Results > OK

```
 PRINT ELEM ELEMENT SOLUTION PER ELEMENT

 ***** POST1 ELEMENT SOLUTION LISTING *****

  LOAD STEP      1  SUBSTEP=       1
  TIME=     1.0000        LOAD CASE=   0

 EL=        1 NODES=       1       2 MAT=       1
 LINK1
   TEMP =     0.00     0.00  FLUENCES = 0.000E+00 0.000E+00
 MFORX= -400.00
 SAXL= -3200.0     EPELAXL=-0.000107 EPTHAXL= 0.000000 EPSWAXL=
 0.000000 EPINAXL= 0.000000

 EL=        2 NODES=       2       3 MAT=       1
 LINK1
   TEMP =     0.00     0.00  FLUENCES = 0.000E+00 0.000E+00
 MFORX=  500.00
 SAXL=  4000.0     EPELAXL= 0.000133 EPTHAXL= 0.000000 EPSWAXL=
 0.000000 EPINAXL= 0.000000
```

This file gives the input parameters for each element as well as the computed results. **MFORX** is the **axial force**, and **SAXL** is the **axial stress**. Element (1) is in compression (-400 lbf, -3200 psi) and element (2) is in tension (500 lbf, 4000 psi) as anticipated.

The stress values are well below yield strengths of commonly used steels, but since element (1) is in **compression**, there is the possibility that it could fail by **buckling**. This possibility should be checked.

In the X-Y plane the horizontal link can be considered a pinned end column. Its flexural inertia for buckling in the X-Y plane is $I = 0.0026$ in^4. The Euler pinned-end buckling load is $P_{cr} = \pi^2 EI/L^2 = 1924$ lbf which is greater than the 400 lbf load it is carrying, so it seems OK.

However, the horizontal link could also buckle in the X-Z plane, that is, in a direction normal to the plane of analysis. The end conditions are not pinned for this mode of deformation but probably not quite completely fixed either, so this would require further investigation on the part of the stress analyst.

To obtain the **support reactions**

13. Main Menu > General Postproc > List Results > Reaction Solution > All items > OK

At any point you can **save your work** using the ANSYS **binary file format**. To do this

14. Utility Menu > File > Save as Jobname.db

Your work is saved in the working directory using the current Jobname. The problem is stored using the default ANSYS file format, and the text file you used to define the problem is really no longer needed. **Reload** this model using **File > Resume Jobname**.

To begin a **NEW PROBLEM** use:

15. Utility Menu > File > Clear & Start New ... > OK > Yes
Otherwise data from the old problem may contaminate the new one.

Figure 1-21 Modified truss.

1-5 TUTORIAL 1B – MODIFIED TRUSS

Suppose we wish to evaluate the performance of a composite tube as a replacement for the steel tension member, element (2) in the truss model above. The elastic modulus of the composite tube material is **1.2 x 10^7 psi**, its Poisson's ratio is **0.3** and the tube has a cross sectional area of **0.35 in^2**.

The model must now include two different materials and two different cross sectional geometric properties. These are included in the text file description of the model using the **mat** and **real** commands to specify which property to use when creating each element.

We also want to know how the structure is effected by a **0.01 inch movement of the upper support point to the left**. This movement can be incorporated in the model as a nonzero displacement boundary condition.

Finally, in doing this computation we will include the Solution and Postprocessing instruction in the text file and not perform those steps interactively as we did in the previous tutorial. The appropriate text file is shown below.

1. Prepare Input File

```
/FILNAM,T1B
/title, Simple Truss w Composite Tube
/prep7

et, 1, link1              ! Element type; no.1 is link1

! Material 1
mp, ex, 1, 3.e7           ! Material Properties: E for material no. 1
mp, prxy, 1, 0.27         ! & poisson's ratio for material no.1

! Material 2
mp, ex, 2, 1.2e7           ! Material Properties: E for material no. 2
mp, prxy, 2, 0.3          ! & poisson's ratio for material no.2


! Cross sectional areas
! First area
r, 1, 0.125               ! Real Constant number 1 is 0.125

! Second area
r, 2, 0.35                ! Real Constant number 2 is 0.35

n, 1,  0.0,  0.0, 0.0     ! Node 1 is located at ( 0.0, 0.0, 0.0)
n, 2, 20.0,  0.0, 0.0
n, 3,  0.0, 15.0, 0.0

! Set properties before creating elements
mat, 1
real, 1
en, 1, 1, 2               ! Element Number 1 connects nodes 1 & 2

mat, 2
real, 2
en, 2, 2, 3
```

```
d, 1, all, 0.              ! All Displacements at node 1 are zero
d, 3, ux, -0.01            ! Horizontal Displacement at node 3 is -0.01
d, 3, uy,  0.              ! Vertical Displacement at node 3 is zero


f, 1, fy, -300.            ! Force at node 1 in y-direction is -300.
f, 2, fy, -300.            ! Force at node 2 in y-direction is -300.

finish

/solu                      ! Select static load solution
antype, static
solve
save
finish

/post1                     ! start the post processor

etable, Force, SMISC, 1    ! Create a table of element axial Forces
etable, Stress, LS, 1      ! Create a table of element Stress values

/output,resultsfile,dat    ! Define a file resultsfile.dat in working
                           ! directory
prnsol,u                   ! Write the nodal solution to resultsfile.dat
presol,smisc,1             ! Write the axial forces solution to
                           ! resultsfile.dat
/output
```

2. Utility Menu > File > Read Input from

3. Postprocessing Follow the steps given in Tutorial 1A to find the new model results.

Also use **List > Results > Element Table Data** to view element **axial forces and stresses**. 'Force' and 'Stress' in the text file above are label names that you can specify.

1-6 TUTORIAL 1C – INTERACTIVE PREPROCESSING

Preprocessing by a text file defining the problem was shown in Tutorials 1A and 1B. The **Preprocessing** can also be performed in an **interactive session**. Next we redo Tutorial 1B, but perform the model creation step using interactive menu picks and data entry.

1. Start ANSYS and set the **jobname** to **Tutorial1C** or something else easy to remember, set the desired **working directory**, and set **Title** to something descriptive.

2. Main Menu > Preferences > Structural > h-method > OK

(Here we are setting the type of problem to be solved and method used. Actually the defaults are Structural and h-Method, so we do this only to introduce the ideas. More on this later.)

Indicate that we will use the link1 element for modeling.

3. Preprocessor > Element Type > Add/Edit/Delete > Add > Structural   Link 2D spar   1 > OK > Close

Figure 1-22 Select element type.

A problem may have more than one kind of element. This establishes Element type reference number 1 as the 2D spar, link1. (If we had some beams, we would add reference number 2 as a beam, etc. Each different type needs an identifying number.)

Enter the element cross sectional areas for the rectangular bar and the circular tube.

4. Main Menu > Preprocessor > Real Constants > Add/Edit/Delete > Add > OK

Figure 1-23 Real constants.

Element Type Reference No. 1

Create Real Constant Set No. 1

Enter **AREA = 0.125** and **ISTRN = 0** (initial strain) for real constant set 1 **OK > Close**

Figure 1-24 Real constant set No. 1.

Figure 1-25 Real constants window.

Add the second element size before closing the Real Constants window   **Add > OK**

Element Type Reference No. 1

Create Real Constant Set No. 2

Enter **AREA = 0.35** and **ISTRN = 0** for real constant set 2 > **OK**

Real Constant Set Number 2, for LINK1	
Element Type Reference No. 1	
Real Constant Set No.	2
Cross-sectional area AREA	0.35
Initial strain ISTRN	
OK Apply Cancel Help	

Figure 1-26 Real constant set No. 2.

(A blank numeric input field is interpreted as a zero.)

Close the Real Constants window which now shows Set 1 and Set 2 > **Close**

Enter the material properties next.

5. Main Menu > Preprocessor > Material Props > Material Models

Material Model Number 1

Double click **Structural > Linear > Elastic > Isotropic**

Figure 1-27 Material models.

Enter **EX = 3.E7** and **PRXY = 0.27 > OK**

Figure 1-28 Properties for material no. 1.

Second material: In the Define Material Model Behavior window, **Material > New Model Define Material ID** > 2

Figure 1-29 Define material ID no. 2.

Enter **EX = 1.2E7** and **PRXY = 0.3 > OK**

Figure 1-30 Properties for material no. 2.

Close the Define Material Model Behavior window.

Now enter **nodal coordinate** data and **element connectivity** information.

6. Main Menu > Preprocessor > Modeling > Create > Nodes > In Active CS

For Node 1: Enter **Node number = 1; X = 0.0, Y = 0.0 > Apply**

Figure 1-31 Create nodes.

For Nodes 2 and 3:

Enter **Node number = 2; X = 20.0, Y = 0.0 > Apply**

Enter **Node number = 3; X = 0.0, Y = 15.0 > OK**

(CS stands for Coordinate System. Because link1 can only be used for a 2D, X-Y plane model, no Z-coordinate values need be entered. It does not hurt anything to add them if you wish however.)

If you make a mistake, return to this Node Create window to correct the coordinate values. You can use **Preprocessor > Modeling > Delete** to remove nodes.

Next select Material Property (1) and Real Property Set (1), then create element (1).

7. Main Menu > Preprocessor > Modeling > Create > Elements > Elem Attributes

Select defaults, Material number > **1** and Real constant set number > **1 > OK**

Figure 1-32 Select element attributes.

Figure 1-33 Element attributes.

8. Main Menu > Preprocessor > Modeling > Create > Elements > Auto Numbered > Thru Nodes

Pick **Node 1** then **Node 2 > OK**

Now select the second set of material and real properties, and create element (2).

9. Main Menu > Preprocessor > Modeling > Create > Elements > Elem Attributes

Select Material number **> 2** and Real constant set number **> 2 > OK**

10. Main Menu > Preprocessor > Modeling > Create > Elements > Auto Numbered > Thru Nodes

Pick **Node 2** then **Node 3 > OK**

In this simple example we have only two elements, and they each have different properties. If several elements have the same material and real properties, you only need to set the properties once, then create all those elements before changing to the next set of material and real properties.

Now let's check the element properties to make sure the input was correct.

11. Utility Menu > List > Elements > Nodes+Attr + RealConst

```
LIST ALL SELECTED ELEMENTS.   (LIST NODES)

   ELEM MAT TYP REL ESY SEC          NODES

      1   1   1   1   0   1      1     2
   AREA          ISTR
  0.125000      0.00000
      2   2   1   2   0   1      2     3
   AREA          ISTR
  0.350000      0.00000
```

The element data is correct, so we can now apply the boundary conditions and loadings, both located under 'Loads' in ANSYS.

12. Main Menu > Preprocessor > Loads > Define Loads > Apply > Structural > Displacement > On Nodes

Pick **Node 1 > OK > All DOF > Constant value > Displacement value = 0 > Apply**

Figure 1-34 Boundary conditions, Node 1.

(A blank entry for value is interpreted as a zero. If you make a mistake, return to this window or use **Loads > Delete . . .** to make corrections.)

For Node 3:

Pick **Node 3 > OK > UX > Constant value >** Enter **–0.01 > Apply**

Apply U,ROT on Nodes

[D] Apply Displacements (U,ROT) on Nodes

Lab2   DOFs to be constrained

All DOF
UX
UY
VELX
VELY

Apply as

Constant value ▼

If Constant value then:

VALUE   Displacement value

-0.01

OK	Apply	Cancel	Help

Figure 1-35 Boundary condition, node 3.

Again pick **Node 3 > OK > UY > Constant value** > Enter **0 > OK**

Finally we will apply the 300 lbf forces.

13. Main Menu > Preprocessor > Loads > Define Loads > Apply > Structural > Force/Moment > On Nodes

Pick Nodes **1** *and* **2**, Select **FY**, and **Constant value**, Enter **–300 > OK**

Apply F/M on Nodes

[F] Apply Force/Moment on Nodes

Lab   Direction of force/mom   FY ▼

Apply as   Constant value ▼

If Constant value then:

VALUE   Force/moment value   -300

OK	Apply	Cancel	Help

Figure 1-36 Loads.

Let's check the boundary conditions and loads. Use the **Utility Menu**, top of the screen.

14. Utility Menu > List > Loads > DOF Constraints > On All Nodes

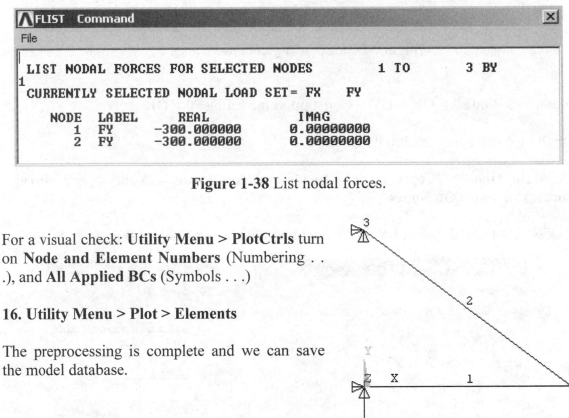

```
┌─────────────────────────────────────────────────────────────────┐
│ Λ DLIST  Command                                              [X] │
├─────────────────────────────────────────────────────────────────┤
│ File                                                              │
├─────────────────────────────────────────────────────────────────┤
│                                                                   │
│  LIST CONSTRAINTS FOR SELECTED NODES           1 TO      3 BY   1 │
│  CURRENTLY SELECTED DOF SET= UX    UY                             │
│                                                                   │
│     NODE  LABEL      REAL              IMAG                       │
│        1  UX       0.00000000        0.00000000                   │
│        1  UY       0.00000000        0.00000000                   │
│        3  UX      -0.100000000E-01   0.00000000                   │
│        3  UY       0.00000000        0.00000000                   │
│                                                                   │
└─────────────────────────────────────────────────────────────────┘
```

Figure 1-37 List constraints.

15. Utility Menu > List > Loads > Forces > On All Nodes

```
┌─────────────────────────────────────────────────────────────────┐
│ Λ FLIST  Command                                             [X]  │
├─────────────────────────────────────────────────────────────────┤
│ File                                                              │
├─────────────────────────────────────────────────────────────────┤
│                                                                   │
│  LIST NODAL FORCES FOR SELECTED NODES          1 TO      3 BY     │
│ 1                                                                 │
│  CURRENTLY SELECTED NODAL LOAD SET= FX    FY                      │
│                                                                   │
│     NODE  LABEL      REAL              IMAG                       │
│        1  FY      -300.000000       0.00000000                    │
│        2  FY      -300.000000       0.00000000                    │
│                                                                   │
└─────────────────────────────────────────────────────────────────┘
```

Figure 1-38 List nodal forces.

For a visual check: **Utility Menu > PlotCtrls** turn on **Node and Element Numbers** (Numbering . . .), and **All Applied BCs** (Symbols . . .)

16. Utility Menu > Plot > Elements

The preprocessing is complete and we can save the model database.

Figure 1-39 Model plot.

17. Utility Menu > File > Save as Jobname.db   (or **Save as . . .** you supply a name.)

1-7 HOW IT WORKS

In finite element analysis or in matrix structural analysis, a matrix is developed to describe the input-output behavior of each element. In this lesson the elements are truss elements, and the behavior we need is the relationship between the nodal loads **f** and the nodal displacements **u**. This matrix is called the **element stiffness matrix**.

To analyze a structure composed of many truss elements, each element stiffness matrix is evaluated according to its length, area, and material modulus of elasticity. Next, a mathematical model of the entire structure is created by assembling the individual element stiffness matrices, much like one builds a mathematical model of an electrical circuit from electrical resistor, capacitor, etc. component models. At a node where two trusses join, the overall stiffness of the assembled structure (resistance to an external force) is increased by the sum of the stiffness of the individual elements that come together at that node. For linear analysis, the resulting global problem is the set of linear algebraic equations shown below.

$$\{P\} = [K] \{U\}$$

For the problem in Tutorial 1A, **{P}** is the vector of external loads **Fx** and **Fy**, **[K]** is the global stiffness matrix assembled from the element stiffness matrices, and **{U}** is the vector of node point displacements **Ux** and **Uy**. **{P}** and **[K]** are known from the definition of the problem under consideration, and **{U}** is to be found by solving the matrix equation above. If the structure can move as a **rigid body** when a force is applied, **[K]** will be singular, and the equations cannot be solved.

An important part of finite element analysis is getting the boundary conditions right. For static loads analysis, the object must have enough of the right kind of displacement constraints to **prevent rigid body motion** as mentioned above. ANSYS may provide a warning or error message if the model is **under constrained** because of the singular stiffness matrix or it may make an attempt to solve the problem and compute displacements which are unreasonably large, on the order of 10^6 or greater. Remove one of the supports in Tutorial 1A and see what happens.

On the other hand, the model must be properly constrained so it does not have boundary conditions that define a problem other than the one you really want to solve.

1-8 SUMMARY

Simple 2-D truss models were used in this lesson to introduce the general form of typical FEM models, to introduce basic ANSYS operations, to demonstrate both file-based and interactive analysis options, and to introduce some facets of the important engineering modeling decisions that must be considered in finite element analysis. Explanations of the use of gravity loadings and multiple load cases are presented in Lesson 9.

In Lesson 2 we consider problems in Plane Stress and Plane Strain wherein models of solid parts are developed using two-dimensional triangular or quadrilateral elements developed for that purpose. Modeling of this nature gives us the ability to consider complex geometries, boundary conditions and loadings that may occur in everyday engineering practice.

1-9 PROBLEMS

You can use the start-up dialog box or **File > Change Title** to add the problem number and your name to the title that appears on all plots associated with a particular job.

1-1 The truss shown has a horizontal joint spacing of 9 ft and a vertical joint spacing of 6 ft. It is made of steel pin-jointed tubes whose cross sections are 6.625 in outer diameter with a 0.28 wall thickness. Find the maximum displacement, the maximum stress and determine if any of the members in compression are likely to buckle. The vertical force is 50,000 lbf.

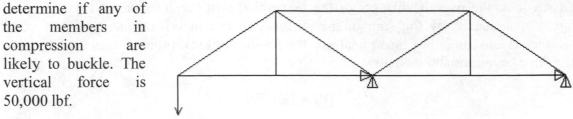

Figure P1-1

1-2 Solve problem 1-1 again but change the horizontal and vertical elements to aluminum tubes with a 8.625 inch OD and a 0.322 inch wall thickness.

1-3 The truss shown is made of steel from pin-jointed elements that have a square cross section 15 mm on a side. The horizontal joint spacing is 2 m. The vertical spacing is 4 m and 2 m. The downward load is 3000 N. Find the maximum displacement, the highest stressed element, and evaluate the possibility of buckling.

F

Figure P1-3

1-4 Solve problem 1-3 if the three horizontal members are made of aluminum with a 20 mm x 20 mm square cross section.

1-5 Find the magnitude and location of the maximum displacement and the maximum stress in the 2-D model of a pin jointed tower shown below. All elements are 4 x 4 x 3/8 steel angle sections with area 2.86 sq in. The load **P** has a value equal to 4500 lbf.

Are any elements likely to buckle if the section minimum flexural inertia is 2.1 in^4?

Figure P1-5

1-6 The truss in figure P1-6 is made from steel elements with 2 inch diameter solid circular cross sections. The horizontal spacing is 40 ft, the vertical spacing from the supports up is 30 ft., 40 ft., and 60 ft. A downward load of 1000 lbf is applied at each of the upper nodes. Find the maximum stress and deflection.

Figure P1-6

NOTES:

Lesson 2

Plane Stress
Plane Strain

2-1 OVERVIEW

Plane stress and plane strain problems are an important subclass of general three-dimensional problems. The tutorials in this lesson demonstrate:

- ♦ Solving planar stress concentration problems.

- ♦ Evaluating potential inaccuracies in the solutions.

- ♦ Using the various ANSYS 2D element formulations.

2-2 INTRODUCTION

It is possible for an object such as the one on the cover of this book to have six components of stress when subjected to arbitrary three-dimensional loadings. When referenced to a Cartesian coordinate system these components of stress are:

Normal Stresses σ_x, σ_y, σ_z

Shear Stresses τ_{xy}, τ_{yz}, τ_{zx}

Figure 2-1 Stresses in 3 dimensions.

In general, the analysis of such objects requires three-dimensional modeling as discussed in Lesson 4. However, two-dimensional models are often easier to develop, easier to solve and can be employed in many situations **if** they can accurately represent the behavior of the object under loading.

A state of **Plane Stress** exists in a thin object loaded in the plane of its largest dimensions. Let the *X-Y* plane be the plane of analysis. The non-zero stresses σ_x, σ_y, and τ_{xy} lie in the *X - Y* plane and do not vary in the *Z* direction. Further, the other stresses (σ_z, τ_{yz}, and τ_{zx})are all zero for this kind of geometry and loading. A thin beam loaded in its plane and a spur gear tooth are good examples of plane stress problems.

ANSYS provides a 6-node planar triangular element along with 4-node and 8-node quadrilateral elements for use in the development of plane stress models. We will use both triangles and quads in solution of the example problems that follow.

2-3 PLATE WITH CENTRAL HOLE

To start off, let's solve a problem with a known solution so that we can check our computed results and understanding of the FEM process. The problem is that of a tensile-loaded thin plate with a central hole as shown in Figure 2-2.

Figure 2-2 Plate with central hole.

The **1.0 m x 0.4 m** plate has a **thickness** of **0.01 m**, and a central hole **0.2 m** in **diameter**. It is made of steel with material properties; **elastic modulus**, $E = 2.07 \times 10^{11}$ N/m^2 and **Poisson's ratio,** $v = 0.29$. We apply a horizontal tensile loading in the form of a pressure $p = -1.0$ N/m^2 along the vertical edges of the plate.

Because holes are necessary for fasteners such as bolts, rivets, etc, the need to know stresses and deformations near them occurs very often and has received a great deal of study. The results of these studies are widely published, and we can look up the stress concentration factor for the case shown above. Before the advent of suitable computation methods, the effect of most complex stress concentration geometries had to be evaluated experimentally, and many available charts were developed from experimental results.

The uniform, homogeneous plate above is symmetric about horizontal axes in both geometry and loading. This means that the state of stress and deformation below a horizontal centerline is a mirror image of that above the centerline, and likewise for a vertical centerline. We can take advantage of the symmetry and, by applying the correct boundary conditions, use only a quarter of the plate for the finite element model. For small problems using symmetry may not be too important; for large problems it can save modeling and solution efforts by eliminating one-half or a quarter or more of the work.

Place the origin of *X-Y* coordinates at the center of the hole. If we pull on both ends of the plate, points on the centerlines will move along the centerlines but not perpendicular to them. This indicates the appropriate displacement conditions to use as shown below.

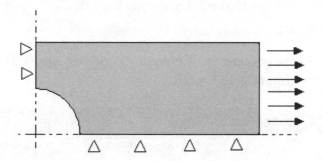

Figure 2-3 Quadrant used for analysis.

In Tutorial 2A we will use ANSYS to determine the maximum horizontal stress in the plate and compare the computed results with the maximum value that can be calculated using tabulated values for stress concentration factors. Interactive commands will be used to formulate and solve the problem.

2-4 TUTORIAL 2A - PLATE

Objective: Find the **maximum axial stress** in the plate with a central hole and compare your result with a computation using published stress concentration factor data.

PREPROCESSING

1. Start ANSYS, select the **Working Directory** where you will store the files associated with this problem. Also set the **Jobname** to **Tutorial2A** or something memorable and provide a **Title**.

(If you want to make changes in the Jobname, working Directory, or Title after you've started ANSYS, use **File > Change Jobname** or **Directory** or **Title**.)

Select the six node triangular element to use for the solution of this problem.

Figure 2-4 Six-node triangle.

2. Main Menu > Preprocessor > Element Type > Add/Edit/Delete > Add > Structural Solid > Quad 8node 183 > OK

Figure 2-5 Element selection.

Select the **option** where you define the plate thickness.

3. Options (Element shape K1) **> Triangle,**

      Options (Element behavior K3) **> Plane strs w/thk > OK > Close**

Figure 2-6 Element options.

4. **Main Menu > Preprocessor > Real Constants > Add/Edit/Delete > Add > OK**

Figure 2-7 Real constants.

(Enter the plate thickness of 0.01 m.) >Enter **0.01 > OK > Close**

Figure 2-8 Enter the plate thickness.

Enter the material properties.

5. Main Menu > Preprocessor > Material Props > Material Models

Material Model Number 1, Double click **Structural > Linear > Elastic > Isotropic**

Enter **EX = 2.07E11** and **PRXY = 0.29 > OK** (**Close** the Define Material Model Behavior window.)

Create the geometry for the upper right quadrant of the plate by subtracting a 0.2 m diameter circle from a 0.5 x 0.2 m rectangle. Generate the rectangle first.

6. Main Menu > Preprocessor > Modeling > Create > Areas > Rectangle > By 2 Corners

Enter (lower left corner) **WP X = 0.0, WP Y = 0.0** and **Width = 0.5, Height = 0.2 > OK**

7. Main Menu > Preprocessor > Modeling > Create > Areas > Circle > Solid Circle

Enter **WP X = 0.0, WP Y = 0.0** and **Radius = 0.1 > OK**

Figure 2-9 Create areas.

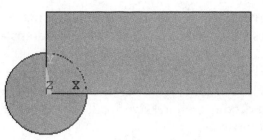

Figure 2-10 Rectangle and circle.

Now **subtract** the circle from the rectangle. (Read the messages in the window at the bottom of the screen as necessary.)

8. Main Menu > Preprocessor > Modeling > Operate > Booleans > Subtract > Areas > Pick the rectangle > OK, then pick the circle **> OK**

Figure 2-11 Geometry for quadrant of plate.

Create a mesh of triangular elements over the quadrant area.

9. Main Menu > Preprocessor > Meshing > Mesh > Areas > Free Pick the quadrant **> OK**

Figure 2-12 Triangular element mesh.

Apply the displacement boundary conditions and loads to the geometry **lines** instead of the nodes as we did in the previous Lesson.

10. Main Menu > Preprocessor > Loads > Define Loads > Apply > Structural > Displacement > On Lines Pick the left edge of the quadrant **> OK > UX = 0. > OK**

11. Main Menu > Preprocessor > Loads > Define Loads > Apply > Structural > Displacement > On Lines Pick the bottom edge of the quadrant **> OK > UY = 0. > OK**

12. Main Menu > Preprocessor > Loads > Define Loads > Apply > Structural > Pressure > On Lines. Pick the right edge of the quadrant **> OK > Pressure = -1.0 > OK** (A positive pressure would be a compressive load, so we use a *negative* pressure. The pressure is shown by the two arrows.)

Figure 2-13 Model with loading and displacement boundary conditions.

The model-building step is now complete, and we can proceed to the solution. First, to be safe, save the model.

13. Utility Menu > File > Save as Jobname.db   (Or **Save as …. ;** use a new name)

SOLUTION

The interactive solution proceeds as illustrated in the tutorials of Lesson 1.

14. Main Menu > Solution > Solve > Current LS > OK

The **/STATUS Command** window displays the problem parameters and the **Solve Current Load Step** window is shown. Check the solution options in the /STATUS window and if all is OK, select **File > Close**

In the **Solve Current Load Step** window, Select **OK**, and when the solution is complete, **close** the **'Solution is Done!'** window.

POSTPROCESSING

We can now **plot the results** of this analysis and also **list the computed values**. First examine the **deformed shape**.

15. Main Menu > General Postproc > Plot Results > Deformed Shape > Def. + Undef. > OK

```
DISPLACEMENT

STEP=1
SUB =1
TIME=1
DMX =.320E-11

U
```

Figure 2-14 Plot of Deformed shape.

The deformed shape looks correct. (The undeformed shape is indicated by the dashed lines.) The right end moves to the right in response to the tensile load in the x-direction, the circular hole ovals out, and the top moves down because of Poisson's effect. Note that the element edges on the circular arc are represented by straight lines. This is an artifact of the plotting routine not the analysis. The six-node triangle has curved sides, and if you pick on a mid-side of one these elements, you will see that a node is placed on the curved edge.

The maximum displacement is shown on the graph legend as 0.32e-11 which seems reasonable. The units of displacement are meters because we employed meters and N/m^2 in the problem formulation. Now plot the stress in the X direction.

16. **Main Menu > General Postproc > Plot Results > Contour Plot > Element Solu > Stress > X-Component of stress > OK**

Use **PlotCtrls > Symbols [/PSF] Surface Load Symbols** (set to **Pressures**) and **Show pre and convect as** (set to **Arrows**) to display the pressure loads.

[/PSF] Surface Load Symbols	Pressures
Visibility key for shells	☐ Off
Plot symbols in color	☑ On
Show pres and convect as	Arrows

Figure 2-15 Surface load symbols.

Also select **Display All Applied BCs**

ELEMENT SOLUTION

STEP=1
SUB =1
TIME=1
SX   (NOAVG)
RSYS=0
DMX =.321E-11
SMN =-.195677
SMX =4.581

U

PRES-NORM
-1

-.195677   .865802   1.927   2.989   4.05
        .335063   1.397   2.458   3.519   4.581

Figure 2-16 Element SX stresses.

The minimum, **SMN**, and maximum, **SMX,** stresses as well as the color bar legend give an overall evaluation of the SX stress state. We are interested in the maximum stress at the hole. Use the **Zoom** to focus on the area with highest stress. (Your meshes and results may differ a bit from those shown here.)

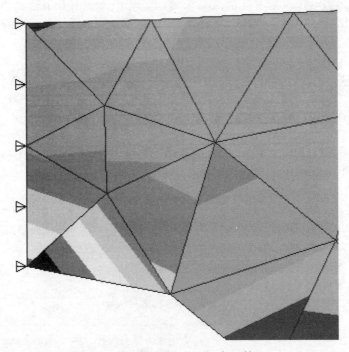

Figure 2-17 SX stress detail.

Stress variations in the actual isotropic, homogeneous plate should be smooth and continuous across elements. The **discontinuities** in the SX stress contours above indicate that the number of elements used in this model is too few to accurately calculate the stress values near the hole because of the stress gradients there. We **will not accept** this stress solution. More six-node elements are needed in the region near the hole to find accurate values of the stress. On the other hand, in the right half of the model, away from the stress riser, the calculated stress contours are smooth, and SX would seem to be accurately determined there.

It is **important** to note that in the plotting we selected **Element Solu** (Element Solution) in order to look for stress contour discontinuities. If you pick **Nodal Solu** to plot instead, for problems like the one in this tutorial, the stress values will be averaged before plotting, and any contour discontinuities (and thus errors) will be hidden. If you plot nodal solution stresses you will always see smooth contours.

A word about **element accuracy:** The FEM implementation of the **truss** element is taken directly from solid mechanics studies, and there is no approximation in the solutions for node-loaded truss structures formulated and solved in the ways discussed in Lesson 1.

The **continuum elements** such as the ones for plane stress and plane strain, on the other hand, are normally developed using displacement functions of a polynomial type to represent the displacements within the element, and the higher the polynomial, the greater the accuracy. The ANSYS six-node triangle uses a quadratic polynomial and is capable of representing linear stress and strain variations within an element.

Near stress concentrations the stress gradients vary quite sharply. To capture this variation, the number of elements near the stress concentrations must be increased proportionately.

To obtain more elements in the model, return to the Preprocessor and refine the mesh, first remove the pressure. All elements are subdivided and the mesh below is created

17. Main Menu > Preprocessor > Loads > Define Loads > Delete > Structural > Pressure > On Lines. Pick the right edge of the quadrant. **Main Menu > Preprocessor > Meshing > Modify Mesh > Refine At > All** (Select **Level of refinement 1.**)

Figure 2-18 Global mesh refinement.

We will also refine the mesh selectively near the hole.

18. Main Menu > Preprocessor > Meshing > Modify Mesh > Refine At > Nodes. (Select the three nodes shown.) **> OK** (Select the **Level of refinement = 1**) **> OK**

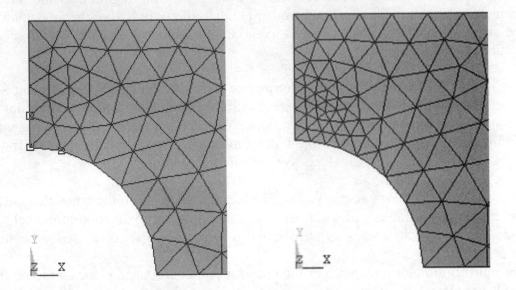

Figure 2-19 Selective refinement at nodes.

(Note: Alternatively you can use **Preprocessor > Meshing > Clear > Areas** to remove all elements and build a completely new mesh. **Plot > Areas** afterwards to view the area again. Note also that too much local refinement can create a mesh with too rapid a transition between fine and coarse mesh regions.)

Now repeat the solution, and replot the stress SX.

19. Main Menu > Solution > Solve > Current LS > OK

Save your work.

20. File > Save as Jobname.db

Plot the stresses in the X-direction.

21. Main Menu > General Postproc > Plot Results > Contour Plot > Element Solu > Stress > X-Component of stress > OK

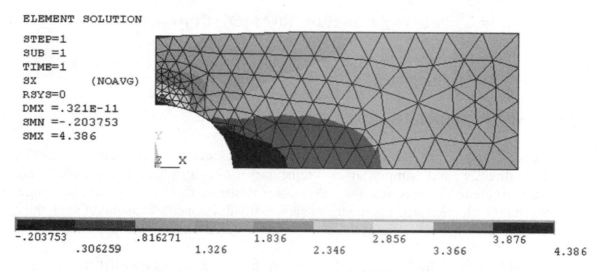

Figure 2-20 SX stress contour after mesh refinement.

Figure 2-21 SX stress detail contour after mesh refinement.

The element solution stress contours are now smooth across element boundaries, and the stress legend shows a maximum value of 4.386 *Pa*, a 4.3 percent change in the computed stress.

To check this result, find the stress concentration factor for this problem in a text or reference book or from a suitable web site. For the geometry of this example we find $K_t =$ 2.17. We can compute the maximum stress using $(K_t)(\text{load})/(\text{net cross sectional area})$. Using the pressure $p = 1.0 \ Pa$ we obtain.

$$\sigma_{x\,MAX} = 2.17 * p * (0.4)(0.01)/[(0.4 - 0.2) * 0.01] = 4.34Pa$$

The computed maximum value is **4.39 *Pa*** which is around **one percent in error**, *assuming* that the value of K_t is exact.

2-5 THE APPROXIMATE NATURE OF FEM

As mentioned above, the stiffness matrix for the truss elements of Lesson 1 can be developed directly and simply from elementary solid mechanics principles. For continuum problems in two and three-dimensional stress, this is generally no longer possible, and the element stiffness matrices are usually developed by assuming something specific about the characteristics of the displacements that can occur within an element.

Ordinarily this is done by specifying the highest degree of the polynomial that governs the displacement distribution within an element. For **h-method** elements, the polynomial degree depends upon the **number of nodes** used to describe the element, and the interpolation functions that relate displacements within the element to the displacements at the nodes are called **shape functions**. In ANSYS, 2-dimensional problems can be modeled with **six-node triangles**, **four-node quadrilaterals** or **eight-node quadrilaterals**.

Figure 2-22 Triangular and quadrilateral elements.

The greater the number of nodes, the higher the order of the polynomial and the greater the accuracy in describing displacements, stresses and strains within the element. If the stress is constant throughout a region, a very simple model is sufficient to describe the stress state, perhaps only one or two elements. If there are gradients in the stress distributions within a region, high-degree displacement polynomials and/or many elements are required to accurately analyze the situation.

These comments explain the variation in the accuracy of the results as different numbers of elements were used to solve the problem in the previous tutorial and why the engineer must carefully prepare a model, start with small models, grow the models as understanding of the problem develops and carefully interpret the calculated results. The ease with which models can be prepared and solved sometimes leads to careless evaluation of the computed results.

2-6 ANSYS FILES

The files created during the solution were saved in step 20 of Tutorial 2A. Look in the working directory and you see Tutorial2A files with extensions **BCS**, **db**, **dbb**, **esav**, **full**, **mntr**, **PVTS**, **rst**, and **stat**. However, the Tutorial 2A problem can be reloaded using only **Tutorial2A.db**, so if you want to save disk space, you can delete the others.

2-7 ANSYS GEOMETRY

The finite element model consists of elements and nodes and is separate from the geometry on which it may be based. It is possible to build the finite element model without consideration of any underlying geometry as was done in the truss examples of Lesson 1, but in many cases, development of the geometry is the first task.

Two-dimensional geometry in ANSYS is built from **keypoints**, **lines** (straight, arcs, splines), and **areas**. These geometric items are assigned numbers and can be listed, numbered, manipulated, and plotted. The keypoints (2,3,4,5,6), lines (2,3,5,9,10), and area (3) for Tutorial 2A are shown below.

Figure 2-23 Keypoints, lines and areas.

The finite element model developed previously for this part used the area A3 for development of the node/element FEM mesh. The loads, displacement boundary conditions and pressures were applied to the geometry lines. When the solution step was executed, the loads were transferred from the lines to the FEM model nodes. Applying boundary conditions and loads to the geometry facilitates remeshing the problem. The geometry does not change, only the number and location of nodes and elements, and at solution time, the loads are transferred to the new mesh.

Geometry can be created in ANSYS interactively (as was done in the previous tutorial) or it can be created by reading a text file. For example, the geometry of Tutorial 2A can be generated with the following text file using the **File > Read Input from** command sequence. (The keypoint, line, etc. numbers will be different from those shown above.)

```
/FILNAM,Geom
/title, Stress Concentration Geometry
! Example of creating geometry using keypoints, lines, arcs
/prep7
! Create geometry
k, 1,  0.0,  0.0        ! Keypoint 1 is at 0.0, 0.0
k, 2,  0.1,  0.0
k, 3,  0.5,  0.0
k, 4,  0.5,  0.2
k, 5,  0.0,  0.2
k, 6,  0.0,  0.1

L, 2, 3                 ! Line from keypoints 2 to 3
L, 3, 4
L, 4, 5
L, 5, 6

! arc from keypoint 2 to 6, center kp 1, radius 0.1
LARC, 2, 6, 1, 0.1

AL, 1, 2, 3, 4, 5    ! Area defined by lines 1,2,3,4,5
```

Geometry for FEM analysis also can be created with solid modeling **CAD** or other software and imported into ANSYS. The **IGES** (Initial Graphics Exchange Specification) neutral file is a common format used to exchange geometry between computer programs. Tutorial 2B demonstrates this option for ANSYS geometry development.

2-8 TUTORIAL 2B – SEATBELT COMPONENT

Objective: Determine the stresses and deformation of the prototype seatbelt component shown in the figure below if it is subjected to tensile load of **1000 lbf**.

Figure 2-24 Seatbelt component.

The seatbelt component is made of steel, has an over all length of about 2.5 inches and is 3/32 = 0.09375 inches thick. A solid model of the part was developed in a CAD system and exported as an IGES file. The file is imported into ANSYS for analysis. For simplicity we will analyze only the right, or 'tongue' portion of the part in this tutorial.

Figure 2-25 Seatbelt 'tongue'.

PREPROCESSING

1. Start ANSYS, Run Interactive, set jobname, and working directory.

Create the top half of the geometry above. The latch retention slot is 0.375 x 0.8125 inches and is located 0.375 inch from the right edge.

If you are not using an IGES file to define the geometry for this exercise, you can create the geometry directly in ANSYS with key points, lines, and arcs by selecting **File > Read Input from** to read in the text file given below and by **skipping the IGES import steps 2, 3, 4, and 10 below.**

```
/FILNAM,Seatbelt
/title, Seatbelt Geometry
! Example of creating geometry using keypoints, lines, arcs
/prep7
! Create geometry
k, 1,  0.0,      0.0          ! Keypoint 1 is at 0.0, 0.0
k, 2,  0.75,     0.0
k, 3,  1.125,    0.0
k, 4,  1.5,      0.0
k, 5,  1.5,      0.5
k, 6,  1.25,     0.75
k, 7,  0.0,      0.75
k, 8,  1.125,    0.375
k, 9,  1.09375,  0.40625
k, 10, 0.8125,   0.40625
k, 11, 0.75,     0.34375
k, 12, 1.25,     0.5
k, 13, 1.09375,  0.375
k, 14, 0.8125,   0.34375
```

```
L, 1, 2                          ! Line from keypoints 1 to 2
L, 3, 4
L, 4, 5
L, 6, 7
L, 7, 1
L, 3, 8
L, 9, 10
L, 11, 2


! arc from keypoint 5 to 6, center kp 12, radius 0.25, etc.
LARC, 5,6, 12, 0.25
LARC, 8, 9, 13, 0.03125
LARC, 10, 11, 14, 0.0625


AL,all                           ! Use all lines to create the area.
```

2. Alternatively, use a solid modeler to create the top half of the component shown above in the X-Y plane and export an IGES file of the part.

To import the IGES file

3. Utility Menu > File > Import > IGES

Select the IGES file you created earlier. Accept the ANSYS import default settings. If you have trouble with the import, select the alternate options and try again. **Defeaturing** is an automatic process to remove inconsistencies that may exist in the IGES file, for example lines that, because of the modeling or the file translation process, do not quite join to digital precision accuracy.

Figure 2-26 IGES import.

Turn the IGES solid model around if necessary so you can easily select the X-Y plane.

4. Utility Menu > PlotCtrls > Pan, Zoom, Rotate > Back, or use the side-bar icon.

Figure 2-27 Seatbelt solid, front and back.

5. Main Menu > Preprocessor > Element Type > Add/Edit/Delete > Add > Solid > Quad 8node   183 > OK (Use the 8-node quadrilateral element for this problem.)

6. Options > Plane strs w/thk > OK > Close

Enter the thickness

7. Main Menu > Preprocessor > Real Constants > Add/Edit/Delete > Add > (Type 1 Plane 183) **> OK > Enter 0.09375 > OK > Close**

Enter the material properties

8. Main Menu > Preprocessor > Material Props > Material Models

Material Model Number 1, Double click **Structural > Linear > Elastic > Isotropic**

Enter **EX = 3.0E7** and **PRXY = 0.3 > OK** (Close Define Material Model Behavior window.)

Now mesh the X-Y plane area. (Turn area numbers on if it helps.)

9. Main Menu > Preprocessor > Meshing > Mesh > Areas > Free. Pick the X-Y planar area **> OK**

IMPORTANT NOTE: The mesh below was developed from an **IGES** geometry file. Using the text file geometry definition, may produce **a much different mesh**. If so, use the **Modify Mesh** refinement tools to obtain a mesh density that produces results with accuracies comparable to those given below. Computed stress values can be surprisingly sensitive mesh differences.

Figure 2-28 Quad 8 mesh.

The IGES solid model is no longer needed, and since its lines and areas may interfere with subsequent modeling operations, we can delete it from the session.

10. Main Menu > Preprocessor > Modeling > Delete > Volume and Below   (Don't be surprised if everything disappears. Just **Plot > Elements** to see the mesh again.)

11. Utility Menu > PlotCtrls > Pan, Zoom, Rotate > Front   (If necessary to see the front side of mesh.)

Figure 2-29 .Mesh, front view.

Now apply displacement and pressure boundary conditions. Zero displacement UX along left edge and zero UY along bottom edge.

12. Main Menu > Preprocessor > Loads > Define Loads > Apply > Structural > Displacement > On Lines Pick the left edge > **UX = 0. > OK**

13. Main Menu > Preprocessor > Loads > Define Loads > Apply > Structural > Displacement > On Lines Pick the lower edge > **UY = 0. > OK**

The 1000 lbf load corresponds to a uniform pressure of about 14,000 psi along the ¾ inch vertical inside edge of the latch retention slot. [1000 lbf/(0.09375 in. x 0.75 in.)].

14. Main Menu > Preprocessor > Loads > Define Loads > Apply > Structural > Pressure > On Lines

Select the inside line and set **pressure = 14000 > OK**

Figure 2-30 Applied displacement and pressure conditions.

Solve the equations.

SOLUTION

15. Main Menu > Solution > Solve > Current LS > OK

POSTPROCESSING

Comparing the **von Mises stress** with the material yield stress is an accepted way of evaluating yielding for **ductile metals** in a combined stress state, so we enter the postprocessor and plot the **element solution** of von Mises stress, **SEQV**.

16. Main Menu > General Postproc > Plot Results > Contour Plot > Element Solu > Stress > (scroll down) von Mises > OK

Zoom in on the small fillet where the maximum stresses occur. The element solution stress contours are reasonably smooth, and the maximum von Mises stress is around **118,000 psi**. Further **mesh refinement** gives a stress value of approximately **140,000 psi**. The small fillet radius of this geometry illustrates the challenges that can arise in creating accurate solutions, however you can easily come within a few percent of the most likely true result using the methods discussed thus far.

Figure 2-31 Von Mises stresses.

Redesign to reduce the maximum stress requires an increase in the thickness or fillet radius. Look at charts of stress concentration factors, and you notice that the maximum stress increases as the radius of the stress raiser decreases, approaching infinite values at zero radii.

If your model has a **zero radius notch**, your finite-size elements will show a very high stress but not infinite stress. If you refine the mesh, the stress will increase but not reach infinity. The finite element technique necessarily describes finite quantities and cannot directly treat an infinite stress at a **singular point**, so don't 'chase a singularity'. If you do not care what happens at the notch (static load, ductile material, etc.) do not worry about this location but examine the stress in other regions.

If you really are concerned about the maximum stress here (fatigue loads or brittle material), then use the actual part notch radius however small (1/32 for this tutorial); do not use a zero radius. Also examine the stress gradient in the vicinity of the notch to make sure the mesh is sufficiently refined near the notch. If a crack tip is the object of the analysis, you should look at fracture mechanics approaches to the problem. (See ANSYS help topics on fracture mechanics.)

The engineer's responsibility is not only to build useful models, but also to interpret the results of such models in intelligent and meaningful ways. This can often get overlooked in the rush to get answers.

Continue with the evaluation and check the strains and deflections for this model as well.

17. Main Menu > General Postproc > Plot Results > Contour Plot > Element Solu > Strain-total > 1st prin > OK

The maximum principal normal strain value is found to be approximately **0.004 in/in**.

18. Main Menu > General Postproc > Plot Results > Contour Plot > Nodal Solu > DOF Solution > X-Component of displacement > OK

Figure 2-32 UX displacements.

The maximum deflection in the X-direction is about **0.00145 inches** and occurs as expected at the center of the right-hand edge of the latch retention slot.

2-9 MAPPED MESHING

Quadrilateral meshes can also be created by mapping a square with a regular array of cells onto a general quadrilateral or triangular region. To illustrate this, **delete the last line,** AL,all, **from the text file** above so that the **area is not created** (just the lines) and read it into ANSYS. Use **PlotCtrls** to turn **Keypoint Numbering On**. Then use

1. Main Menu > Preprocessor > Modeling > Create > Lines > Lines > Straight Line. Successively pick pairs of keypoints until the four interior lines shown below are created.

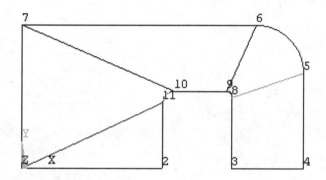

Figure 2-33 Lines added to geometry.

2. Main Menu > Preprocessor > Modeling > Create > Areas > Arbitrary > By Lines Pick the three lines defining the lower left triangular area. > **Apply** > Repeat for the quadrilateral areas. > **Apply > OK**

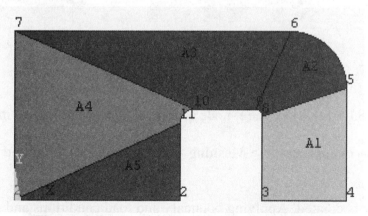

Figure 2-34 Quadrilateral/Triangular regions.

3. Main Menu > Preprocessor > Modeling > Operate > Booleans > Glue > Areas > Pick All

The **glue** operation preserves the boundaries between areas that we will need for mapped meshing.

4. Main Menu > Preprocessor > Meshing > Size Cntrls > ManualSize > Lines > All Lines Enter **4 for NDIV, No. element divisions > OK**

All lines will be divided into four segments for mesh creation.

Element Sizes on Picked Lines

[LESIZE] Element sizes on picked lines

SIZE   Element edge length

NDIV   No. of element divisions   `4`

   (NDIV is used only if SIZE is blank or zero)

KYNDIV SIZE,NDIV can be changed   ☑ Yes

SPACE   Spacing ratio

ANGSIZ Division arc (degrees)

(use ANGSIZ only if number of divisions (NDIV) and

element edge length (SIZE) are blank or zero)

Clear attached areas and volumes   ☐ No

OK   Apply   Cancel   Help

Figure 2-35 Element size on picked lines.

5. Main Menu > Preprocessor > Element Type > Add/Edit/Delete > Add > Solid > Quad 8node   183 > OK (Use the 8-node quadrilateral element for the mesh.)

6. Main Menu > Preprocessor > Meshing > Mesh > Areas > Mapped > 3 or 4 sided > Pick All

The mesh below is created. Applying boundary and load conditions and solving gives the von Mises stress distribution shown. The stress contours are discontinuous because of the poor mesh quality. Notice the long and narrow quads near the point of maximum stress. We need more elements and they need to be better shaped with smaller aspect ratios to obtain satisfactory results.

Figure 2-36 Mapped mesh and von Mises results.

One can tailor the mapped mesh by specifying how many elements are to be placed along which lines. This allows much better control over the quality of the mesh, and an example of using this approach is described in Lesson 4.

2-10 CONVERGENCE

The goal of finite element analysis as discussed in this lesson is to arrive at computed estimates of deflection, strain and stress that converge to definite values as the number of elements in the mesh increases, just as a convergent series arrives at a definite value once enough terms are summed.

For elements based on assumed displacement functions that produce continuum models, the computed displacements are smaller in theory than the true displacements because the assumed displacement functions place an artificial constraint on the deformations that can occur. These constraints are relaxed as the element polynomial is increased or as more elements are used. Thus your computed displacements usually converge smoothly from below to fixed values.

Strains are the x and/or y derivatives of the displacements and thus depend on the distribution of the displacements for any given mesh. The strains and stresses may change in an erratic way as the mesh is refined, first smaller than the final computed values, then larger, etc.

Not all elements are developed using the ideas discussed above, and some will give displacements that converge from above. (See Lesson 6.) In any case you should be alert to computed displacement and stress variations as you perform mesh refinement during the solution of a problem.

2-11 TWO-DIMENSIONAL ELEMENT OPTIONS

The analysis options for two-dimensional elements are: **Plane Stress, Axisymmetric, Plane Strain, Plane Stress with Thickness** and **Generalized Plane Strain**. The two examples thus far in this lesson were of the third type, namely problems of plane stress in which we provided the thickness of the part.

The first analysis option, **Plane Stress**, is the ANSYS default and provides an analysis for a part with **unit thickness**. If you are working on a design problem in which the thickness is not yet known, you may wish to use this option and then select the thickness based upon the stress, strain, and deflection distributions found for a unit thickness.

The second option, **Axisymmetric** analysis is covered in detail in Lesson 3.

Plane Strain occurs in a problem such as a cylindrical roller bearing caged against axial motion and uniformly loaded in a direction normal to the cylindrical surface. Because there is no axial motion, there is no axial strain. Each slice through the cylinder behaves like every other and the problem can be conveniently analyzed with a planar model.

Another plane strain example is that of a long retaining wall, restrained at each end and loaded uniformly by soil pressure on one or both faces.

The **Generalized Plane Strain** feature assumes a finite deformation domain length in the Z direction, as opposed to the infinite value assumed for standard plane strain.

2-12 SUMMARY

Problems of stress concentration in plates subject to in-plane loadings were used to illustrate ANSYS analysis of plane stress problems. Free **triangular** and **quadrilateral** element meshes were developed and analyzed. **Mapped meshing** with quads was also presented. Similar methods are used for solving problems involving plane strain; one only has to choose the appropriate option during element selection. The approach is also applicable to axisymmetric geometries as discussed in the next lesson.

2-13 PROBLEMS

In the problems below, use triangular and/or quadrilateral elements as desired. Triangles may produce more regular shaped element meshes with free meshing. The six-node triangles and eight-node quads can approximate curved surface geometries and, when stress gradients are present, give much better results than the four-node quad elements.

2-1 Find the maximum stress in the aluminum plate shown below. Use tabulated stress concentration factors to independently calculate the maximum stress. Compare the two results by determining the percent difference in the two answers.

Convert the 12 kN concentrated force into an equivalent pressure applied to the edge.

600 mm

75 mm dia

300 mm

12 kN

aluminum plate   10 mm thick

Figure P2-1

2-2 Find the maximum stress for the plate from 2-1 if the hole is located halfway between the centerline and top edge as shown. You will now need to model half of the plate instead of just one quarter and properly restrain vertical rigid body motion. One way to do this is to fix one keypoint along the centerline from UY displacement.

600 mm

75 mm dia

300 mm

12 kN

10 mm thick

Figure P2-2

2-3 An aluminum square 10 inches on a side has a 5-inch diameter hole at the center. The object is in a state of **plane strain** with an internal pressure of 1500 psi. Determine the magnitude and location of the maximum principal stress, the maximum principal strain, and the maximum von Mises stress. Note that no thickness need be supplied for plane strain analysis.

5 inch dia

1500 psi

Figure P2-3   10 x 10 in

2-4 Repeat 2-3 for a steel plate one inch thick in a state of plane stress.

2-5 See if you can reduce the maximum stress for the plate of problem 2-1 by adding holes as shown below. Select a hole size and location that you think will smooth out the 'stress flow' caused by the load transmission through the plate.

600 mm

75 mm dia

300 mm

12 kN

aluminum plate 10 mm thick

Figure P2-5

2-6 Repeat 2-1 but the object is now a plate with notches or with a step in the geometry. (See the next figure.) Select your own dimensions, materials, and loads. Use published stress concentration factor data to compare to your results. The published results are for plates that are relatively long so that there is a uniform state of axial stress at either end relatively far from notch or hole. Create your geometry accordingly.

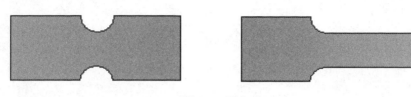

Figure P2-6

2-7 Solve the seatbelt component problem of Tutorial 2B again using six node triangular elements instead of the quadrilaterals. Experiment with mesh refinement. Turn on **Smart Sizing** using size controls to examine the effect on the solution. See if you can compute a maximum von Mises stress of around 140 kpsi.

2-8 Determine the stresses and deflections in an object 'at hand' (such as a seatbelt tongue or retaining wall) whose geometry and loading make it suitable for plane stress or plane strain analysis. Do all the necessary modeling of geometry (use a CAD system if you wish), materials and loadings.

2-9 A cantilever beam with a unit width rectangular cross section is loaded with a uniform pressure along its upper surface. Model the beam as a problem in plane stress. Compute the end deflection and the maximum stress at the cantilever support. Compare your results to those you would find using elementary beam theory.

Figure P2-8

Restrain UX along the cantilever support line, but restrain UY at only one keypoint along this line. Otherwise, the strain in the Y direction due to the Poisson effect is prevented here, and the root stresses are different from elementary beam theory because of the singularity created. (Try fixing all node points in UX and UY and see what happens.)

Select your own dimensions, materials, and pressure. Try a beam that's long and slender and one that's short and thick. The effect of shear loading becomes more important in the deflection analysis as the slenderness decreases.

NOTES:

Lesson 3

Axisymmetric Problems

3-1 OVERVIEW

Axisymmetric Analysis - A problem in which the geometry, loadings, boundary conditions and materials are symmetric with respect to an axis is one that can be solved with an axisymmetric finite element model. The tutorial in this lesson discusses

♦ Creating model geometry using an IGES file or a text file

♦ Evaluating the response of a vessel to an internal pressure

3-2 INTROUCTION

For problems that are rotationally symmetric about an axis, a slicing plane that contains the symmetry axis exposes the interior configuration of the geometry. Since any slice created by such a plane looks like any other slice, the problem can be conveniently analyzed by considering any one planar section as shown in the figure below.

Figure 3-1 Axisymmetric problem.

3-3 CYLINDRICAL PRESSURE VESSEL

A steel pressure vessel with planar ends is subjected to an **internal pressure of 35 MPa** (35 x 10^6 N per m^2). The vessel has an **outer diameter of 200 mm**, an over-all **length of 400 mm** and a **wall thickness of 25 mm**. There is a **25 mm fillet radius** where the interior wall surface joins the end cap as shown in the figure below.

The vessel has a longitudinal axis of rotational symmetry and is also symmetric with respect to a plane passed through it at mid-height. Thus the analyst need consider only the top or bottom half of the vessel.

Figure 3-2 Cylindrical pressure vessel.

The global **Y**-axis is the **ANSYS default axis of symmetry for axisymmetric problems**, and **X** is aligned with the radial direction. The **radial stresses** are labeled **SX**, and the **axial stresses** are labeled **SY**. When the vessel is pressurized, it will expand creating stresses in the **circumferential** or **hoop** direction. These are labeled **SZ**.

A ninety-degree slice of the top half of the vessel is created in the **X-Y plane** in a solid modeler for import as an **IGES file** into ANSYS. IGES is a neutral CAD format file definition. Each software manufacturer writes software for translating from IGES to its native file format and vice versa. The angular extent of the slice is not important; we just want to expose the X-Y plane for analysis. (See the instructions below if you want to create the geometry using ANSYS commands instead of using an IGES file from a solid modeler.)

Figure 3-3 Solid model.

The material properties for the vessel are elastic modulus E = 200 GPa (2 x 10^11 N per m^2), Poisson's ratio = 0.3, Yield strength = 330 MPa (330 x 10^6 N per m^2). The geometric modeling was performed using mm as units of length, so we will use a consistent set of units with $E = 2 \times 10^5$ N per mm^2 and **Yield strength = 330 N per mm^2**. An internal **pressure of 35 N per mm^2** will be used. Results calculated with these inputs will have displacements in mm and stresses in N per mm^2 (MPa).

3-4 TUTORIAL 3A – PRESSURE VESSEL

Objective: Determine if yielding will occur in the cylindrical pressure vessel described above if it is pressurized as indicated.

PREPROCESSING

1. Start ANSYS; set the working directory and job name as usual. First develop the geometry for the vessel cross section.

If you are not using an IGES file to define the geometry for this exercise, you can create the 2D cross section geometry directly in ANSYS with key points, lines, and arcs by selecting File > Read Input from and reading the text file below.

```
/FILNAM,Tutorial3A
/title, Pressure Vessel Geometry
/prep7
! Create geometry

k, 1,  75.,   0.          ! Keypoint 1 is at 75.0, 0.0
k, 2, 100.,   0.
k, 3, 100., 200.
k, 4,   0., 200.
k, 5,   0., 175.
k, 6,  50., 175.
k, 7,  75., 150.
k, 8,  50., 150.


L, 7, 1                   ! Line from keypoints 7 to 1
L, 1, 2
L, 2, 3
L, 3, 4
L, 4, 5
L, 5, 6

larc, 7, 6, 8, 25.        ! Fillet arc

AL, 1, 2, 3, 4, 5, 6, 7  ! Area defined by lines 1 thru 7
```

Skip to the element selection phase, step 4 below.

Alternatively, import the IGES file of the vessel slice.
The **results shown** in this tutorial were created using an imported **IGES file** from Pro/E.

Figure 3-4 Solid in ANSYS

2. Utility Menu > File > Import > IGES Select the IGES file you created earlier. Accept the ANSYS import default settings. If you have trouble with the import, select the alternate options and try again. Defeaturing is an automatic process to remove inconsistencies that may exist in the IGES file such as lines that, because of modeling or the translation process, do not quite join.

Turn the solid model around to show the X-Y plane (Ctrl-Right mouse)

3. Utility Menu > PlotCtrls > Pan, Zoom, Rotate > Back

Figure 3-5 X-Y plane of cross section.

Select the **six-node triangular element** for this analysis and choose the **axisymmetric** modeling option.

4. Main Menu > Preprocessor > Element Type > Add/Edit/Delete >Add > Structural Solid > Quad 8node 183 > OK

5. Options (Element shape K1) > **Triangle,**

       Options (Element behavior K3) > **Axisymmetric > OK > Close**

Enter the material properties

6. Main Menu > Preprocessor > Material Props > Material Models

Material Model Number 1, Double click **Structural > Linear >Elastic > Isotropic**

Enter **EX = 2.0E5** and **PRXY = 0.3 > OK**

Now mesh the X-Y plane area. (Turn area numbers on; **Plot > Areas**; then to select an area, click its number. Use **Cntl + Mouse** buttons to dynamically manipulate the image.)

7. Main Menu > Preprocessor > Meshing > Mesh > Areas > Free Pick the cross section area in the X-Y plane > **OK** (Skip to Step 10 if you are not using an IGES file.)

Figure 3-6 Initial mesh.

The IGES solid model is no longer needed and should be deleted so its lines and areas will not interfere with subsequent operations.

8. Main Menu > Preprocessor > Modeling > Delete > Volume and Below   (Don't be surprised if everything disappears. Just **Plot > Elements** to see the mesh again.)

9. Utility Menu > PlotCtrls > Pan, Zoom, Rotate > Front   (To see the front side of the mesh.)

Increase the mesh density to obtain good accuracy in the solution.

10. Main Menu > Preprocessor > Meshing > Modify Mesh > Refine At > All > Level of Refinement 2 > OK

Figure 3-7 Refined mesh.

Apply displacement and pressure boundary conditions. Select the bottom horizontal edge and restrain it from UY movement.

11. Main Menu > Preprocessor > Loads > Define Loads > Apply > Structural > Displacement > On Lines Pick the lower edge > **UY = 0. > OK**

No displacement constraint is required on the top left vertical edge since it is on the axis of symmetry and axisymmetric modeling prevents any radial motion here.

Apply a pressure to the inside of the cylinder.

12. Main Menu > Preprocessor > Loads > Define Loads > Apply > Structural > Pressure > On Lines

Select the interior lines and set **pressure = 35 > OK**

Figure 3-8 Loads and boundary conditions.

(The pressure may show as single or multiple arrows depending upon the solution stage. If you lose it completely, it will resurface during solution or do a **Utility Menu >Loads > List.**)

SOLUTION

13. Main Menu > Solution > Solve > Current LS > OK

POSTPROCESSING

We can now **plot the results** of this analysis and **list the computed values**.

14. Main Menu > General Postproc > Plot Results > Contour Plot > Element Solu > Stress > von Mises stress > OK

A maximum von Mises stress of just over 200 N per mm^2 (200MPa) is computed at the fillet where the interior sidewall and top join. (Your meshes and results may differ a bit from those shown.)

Figure 3-9 Von Mises Stress on deformed shape.

The deformed shape looks correct, so let's look more closely at the computed solution.

Theoretical Solution

The stresses at points removed from the stress concentration at the end caps (say at the bottom of the vessel segment shown in the figure above) could be predicted using thick walled cylinder theory. For the geometry and loading of this example, theory predicts the following stress components at the **inner surface** of the cylinder.

$$\text{Radial Stress (SX)} = -35 \text{ N per mm}^2$$

$$\text{Axial Stress (SY)} = 45 \text{ N per mm}^2$$

$$\text{Hoop Stress (SZ)} = 125 \text{ N per mm}^2$$

$$\text{Radial Deflection} = 0.0458 \text{ mm}$$

These theoretical results can be used to evaluate the ANSYS solution. Zoom in on the **bottom portion** of the model. Also turn the node numbering on and plot the elements.

The **element solution** plot of the von Mises stress shows smooth contours indicating a reasonably accurate solution, so we can safely use **nodal solution stress values**. List the values for node 20. (The node numbers in your model will depend upon the model building and meshing sequence you use and may be different from what is shown here.)

Figure 3-10 Model detail.

15. Main Menu > General Postproc > List Results > Nodal Solution > Stress > X-Component of stress > OK

```
PRINT S    NODAL SOLUTION PER NODE

***** POST1 NODAL STRESS LISTING *****
PowerGraphics Is Currently Enabled

LOAD STEP=     1  SUBSTEP=        1
  TIME=    1.0000        LOAD CASE=   0
NODAL RESULTS ARE FOR MATERIAL   1

THE FOLLOWING X,Y,Z VALUES ARE IN GLOBAL COORDINATES

   NODE     SX          SY          SZ          SXY
. . . . . .
     20  -34.846      46.440      127.37     -0.18278E-01
. . . . . .
```

The computed values for SX, SY and SZ are only a few percent different from the theoretical solution. (Your numerical values may be slightly different from those shown above.) This correlation gives us confidence in the solution, and if we refine the mesh in this area, closer agreement in the radial (SX) and hoop (SZ) stresses could be obtained. The theoretical solution for the axial stress (SY) is an average value (P/A), so some disagreement is to be expected, and the finite element solution probably gives a better picture of the true stress distribution. (The shear stresses SYZ and SXZ are zero for axisymmetric problems and were deleted from the listing above to save space.) We also check the radial displacement result.

16. Main Menu > General Postproc > List Results > Nodal Solu > DOF Solution > X-Component of displacement > OK

```
PRINT U    NODAL SOLUTION PER NODE

***** POST1 NODAL DEGREE OF FREEDOM LISTING *****

LOAD STEP=      1  SUBSTEP=        1
  TIME=     1.0000      LOAD CASE=   0

THE FOLLOWING DEGREE OF FREEDOM RESULTS ARE IN GLOBAL
COORDINATES

   NODE        UX
. . . .
     20  0.46524E-01
. . . .
```

The computed radial displacement at node 20 is only 0.77 percent different from the theoretical.

To evaluate the possibility of **yielding** for this ductile material we compare the **von Mises** stress to the material yield strength. The maximum vessel stresses occur at the fillet where the vertical wall and the end caps join. Zoom in on an **element solution plot** of SEQV in the vicinity of the fillet, and we see that the stress contours are not completely smooth; there are discontinuities between elements. To get better accuracy, remove the pressure and refine the mesh using the fillet geometry to indicate the region to be refined.

17. Main Menu > Preprocessor > Loads > Define Loads > Delete > Structural > Pressure > On Lines   Main Menu > Preprocessor > Meshing > Modify Mesh > Refine At > Lines (Select the fillet.) **Level = 1 > OK**

(To get a clearer view of the node numbers, you can turn off the MX, MN symbols **PlotCtrls > Window Controls > Window Options > MINM Min-Max Symbols > Off > OK**)

Figure 3-11 SEQV in fillet before and after refinement.

The maximum von Mises stress occurs at the location shown with a value of about **205 N per mm^2**. Comparing this with the yield strength of 330 N per mm^2, we conclude that yielding is not a problem at the fillet for this loading.

Use the **Results Viewer** to inquire further at the point of maximum von Mises stress.

18. Main Menu > Postproc > Results Viewer

19. Choose a result item > Element Solution > Stress > von Mises.

20. Select **Contour**. | von Mises stress   ▼ | Contour ▼ |

21. Click on the first icon, **Plot Results**, 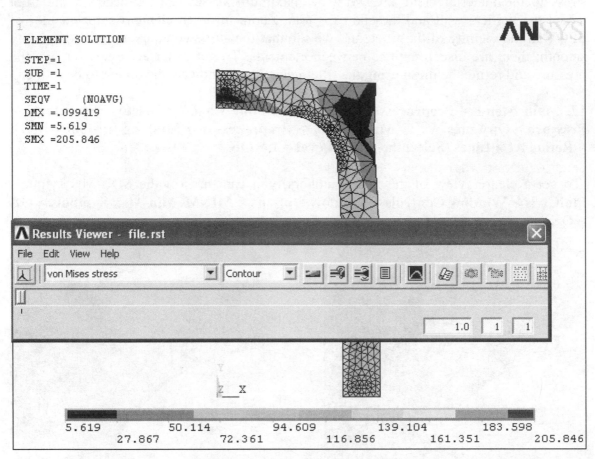; the figure below is displayed.

ELEMENT SOLUTION

STEP=1
SUB =1
TIME=1
SEQV   (NOAVG)
DMX =.099419
SMN =5.619
SMX =205.846

Results Viewer - file.rst

File   Edit   View   Help

von Mises stress ▼   Contour ▼

1.0   1   1

5.619   50.114   94.609   139.104   183.598
     27.867   72.361   116.856   161.351   205.846

Figure 3-12 Results viewer.

22. Zoom in on the region of maximum stress, then click on the **second icon**, **Query Results** and click on the node where the maximum value is indicated. The figure to the right is shown.

The query value is about 204 MPa.

Figure 3-13 Query results, element solution.

Query Subgrid Results

⦿ Pick   ○ Unpick

NODE No. =   998

Global X =   69.5897

       Y =   168.504

       Z =   0

SEQV = 204.36

☐ generate 3D Anno

OK	Apply
Reset	Cancel
Min	Max
Help	

'**Multiple items at this location**' may be shown in a multiple entities window because there are three elements that join at this node, and different stress levels may be calculated in each element. For a continuum problem such the one we are analyzing here, the magnitude of difference in element solution quantities is an indication of the potential error in the solution.

23. OK > Close

Now from the pull-down list in the **Results Viewer** select **Nodal Solution** (instead of Element Solution) > **Stress** > **von Mises**. **Plot Results**, then **Query Results** again at the point of maximum stress.

(To return to the ANSYS main menu, close the Results Viewer window when you are finished.)

Figure 3-14 Query results, nodal solution

The nodal solution magnitudes are the average values computed using quantities calculated for each element connected to the node. Thus the nodal solution contours are always nice and smooth. They give a good representation of stress variations once the mesh is sufficiently dense to produce small differences in quantities calculated for elements with common nodes. (Your results might differ slightly from those shown here.)

3-5 OTHER ELEMENTS

We used triangular elements for meshing in the examples above, but the axisymmetric option is also available with the other two-dimensional ANSYS elements; the four-node quadrilateral (42 or 182) and the eight-node quadrilateral (82 or 183). Quadrilateral elements sometimes offer advantages over triangles when developing mapped meshes or when rectangular or trapezoidal areas can be identified for free meshing. For arbitrary shapes, free triangular meshes may produce more regular shaped elements than free quad meshes. **Smart Size** controls also can be used very effectively to control mesh quality (see Lesson 4).

3-6 SUMMARY

A pressure vessel was used as an example of a problem with symmetry in geometry, boundary conditions, loadings, and material properties about a central axis. An upset shaft in tension is one of many other cases in which simple two-dimensional models may be used to great advantage in the solution of important engineering problems possessing symmetry. The problems below further explore this type of modeling process.

3-7 PROBLEMS

3-1 The steel pressure vessel shown has an internal pressure of 4000 psi. The overall length is 50 inches with inside and outside radii of 5 and 10 inches respectively. Compare the computed stress components at the mid section to theoretical values. Also determine if the vessel will yield with the given internal pressure if its yield strength is 50 kpsi.

Figure P3-1

3-2 Determine the stresses and deflections of the vessel geometry of problem 3-1 if the dimensions are measured in cm and it is subjected to an **external pressure** corresponding to submersion in 100 m of water.

3-3 Compute the maximum tensile stress in a circular shaft with an upset shoulder under **axial loading**. Compare your results to those one can compute using tabulated stress concentration factors for this geometry. Select your own diameters, fillet radius, length, materials, and loads.

Figure P3-3

3-4 The anchor device below is loaded by an axial force of 10,000 lbs. Dimensions shown are in inches. Apply the force as a pressure to the top surface. The base is buried so that its upper surface cannot move in the Y direction and its vertical edge surface cannot move radially.

Select a gray cast iron from which to make the part and find its material properties. Use the maximum normal stress theory of failure to determine if failure is likely to occur in this part. That is, compare the maximum computed principal tensile stress, **S1**, with the material ultimate strength. Use **General Postprocessor > Plot Results > Vector Plots > Predefined > Stress Principal** and sketch the fracture plane if failure were to occur. The groove is 0.20 inch in **diameter**.

Figure P3-4

3-5 A circular aluminum plate 1 m in diameter and 5 cm in thickness is loaded by a uniform pressure of 0.5 Pa distributed over a 0.25 m diameter circle at the center of the plate. The outer edges of the plate are completely fixed from motion. Find the maximum deflection and von Mises stress and their locations.

3-6 Solve 3-5 again if the plate thickness varies from 4 cm at the outer edge to a constant 7 cm over the 0.25 m central circle.

3-7 Compute the magnitude of the maximum radial deflection and the maximum stresses in a hollow sphere with internal/and or external pressure. Select your own dimensions, materials and pressures. Compare your results with published theoretical values. You can create a quadrant of the section using the ANSYS commands **Preprocessor > Create > Circle > Partial Annulus**.

Lesson 4

3-Dimensional Problems

4-1 OVERVIEW

Three-Dimensional Analysis - Problems that do not have an appropriate structural, plane stress, plane strain or axisymmetric model must be solved as three-dimensional problems. Lesson 4 discusses:

- ♦ Developing 3-D models from solid modelers.

- ♦ Meshing volumes with tetrahedron or brick elements.

- ♦ Using cyclic symmetry modeling when applicable.

4-2 INTRODUCTION

Three-dimensional regions that define mechanical parts are often solved using solid tetrahedron or brick elements when simpler models are not available or sometimes when the development of a simpler model involves an excessive commitment of engineering time.

In this lesson we will revisit the pressure vessel of Lesson 3, treating it as a three-dimensional problem instead of an axisymmetric problem. We create the ANSYS model geometry by importing the IGES file of the pressure vessel that was created in a solid modeler. We also give instructions for creating this volume directly in ANSYS in case you are not using a solid modeler in conjunction with this exercise.

4-3 CYLINDRICAL PRESSURE VESSEL

Figure 4-1 shows the cylindrical pressure vessel of Lesson 3. Even though we are going to use three-dimensional modeling for this analysis, we can still take advantage of symmetry to reduce the size of the model that must be analyzed.

Figure 4-1 Cylindrical pressure vessel.

We will use the 90-degree segment of the solid model of the vessel as we did in Lesson 3. The symmetric nature of the geometry and loading means that displacements are zero in directions normal to the faces exposed by the vertical and horizontal cuts employed to create this one-eighth segment of the cylinder.

Figure 4-2 Solid.

4-4 TUTORIAL 4A – PRESSURE VESSEL

Objective: Analyze the pressure vessel as a three dimensional solid using ten-node tetrahedron elements. Compare computed results with thick walled cylinder theory and the maximum von Mises stress with that calculated using the axisymmetric model of Lesson 3.

Figure 4-3 10-node tet.

PREPROCESSING

1. Start ANSYS; set the working directory and job name as usual.

2. If you are not using an IGES file to define the geometry for this exercise, you can create the geometry directly in ANSYS with key points, lines, and arcs by selecting **File > Read Input from** and reading the text file below (then skip step 3).

```
/FILNAM,Tutorial4A
/title, Pressure Vessel Geometry
/prep7
```

```
! Create geometry

k,  1,   75.,    0.          ! Keypoint 1 is at 75.0, 0.0
k,  2,  100.,    0.
k,  3,  100.,  200.
k,  4,    0.,  200.
k,  5,    0.,  175.
k,  6,   50.,  175.
k,  7,   75.,  150.
k,  8,   50.,  150.


L,  7,  1                    ! Line from keypoints 7 to 1
L,  1,  2
L,  2,  3
L,  3,  4
L,  4,  5
L,  5,  6


larc, 7, 6, 8, 25.          ! Fillet arc

AL, 1, 2, 3, 4, 5, 6, 7   ! Area defined by lines 1 thru 7
! rotate the area about k4-k5 axis through 90 deg.

vrotat, all, , , , , , , 4, 5, 90.
```

Alternatively, import the IGES file for the 90-degree segment of the pressure vessel.

3. Utility Menu > File > Import > IGES Select the IGES file you created earlier. Accept the ANSYS import default settings. If you have trouble with the import, select the alternate options and try again. **Defeaturing** is an automatic process to remove inconsistencies that may exist in the IGES file because of modeling or the IGES translation process. (**Ctrl-Right** mouse button to spin the volume.)

Select the **10-node tetrahedron** element (number 187 in the ANSYS menu) for this analysis. The 10-node tets have mid-side nodes to facilitate modeling curved surfaces.

4. Main Menu > Preprocessor > Element Type > Add/Edit/Delete > Add > Solid > Tet 10 node   187 > OK

Enter the material properties

5. Preprocessor > Material Props > Material Models

Material Model Number 1, Double click **Structural > Linear > Elastic > Isotropic**

Enter **EX = 2.0E5** and **PRXY = 0.3 > OK**

Figure 4-4 Solid in ANSYS.

Now use the default settings to mesh the volume that has been created or imported.

6. Main Menu > Preprocessor > Meshing > Mesh > Volumes > Free Pick the solid. > **OK**

Figure 4-5 Initial tetrahedron mesh.

Now apply the displacement boundary conditions. We will apply these to the boundary faces of the solid to facilitate mesh modification operations. Displacements perpendicular to the left, right, and bottom faces exposed by the planes of symmetry must be zero. Use **PlotCtrls > Numbering > Node numbers > On > OK**. Plot Areas and pick the Area No.

7. Main Menu > Preprocessor > Loads > Define Loads > Apply > Structural > Displacement > On Areas Pick the exposed face on the right. > **OK** > **UX = 0.** > **OK**

8. Main Menu > Preprocessor > Loads > Define Loads > Apply > Structural > Displacement > On Areas Pick the exposed face on the left. > **OK** > **UZ = 0.** > **OK**

Figure 4-6 The UX = 0 and UZ = 0 faces.

Set UY = 0 on the bottom face. Use **control + right mouse** to dynamically rotate object so you can see the bottom face.

9. Main Menu > Preprocessor > Loads > Define Loads > Apply > Structural > Displacement > On Areas Pick the bottom face. **> OK > UY = 0. > OK**

Apply the pressure to the inside of the cylinder

10. Main Menu > Preprocessor > Loads > Define Loads > Apply > Structural > Pressure > On Areas Select the three areas that make up the inside surface. **> OK** Set **pressure = 35 > OK**

Figure 4-7 The UY = 0 and applied pressure faces.

Check your work by listing the loads

11. Utility Menu > List > Loads > DOF Constraints > On All Areas

12. Utility Menu > List > Loads > Surface > On All Areas

You can also check the model size while in the Preprocessor

13. Utility Menu > List > Other > Database Summary

```
*** ANSYS GLOBAL STATUS ***

TITLE =
NUMBER OF ELEMENT TYPES =        1
    879 ELEMENTS CURRENTLY SELECTED.  MAX ELEMENT NUMBER =       879
   1817 NODES CURRENTLY SELECTED.     MAX NODE NUMBER =         1817
     17 KEYPOINTS CURRENTLY SELECTED. MAX KEYPOINT NUMBER =      181
     18 LINES CURRENTLY SELECTED.     MAX LINE NUMBER =           98
      8 AREAS CURRENTLY SELECTED.     MAX AREA NUMBER =           16
      1 VOLUMES CURRENTLY SELECTED.   MAX VOL. NUMBER =            1
```

```
MAXIMUM LINEAR PROPERTY NUMBER      =       1
ACTIVE COORDINATE SYSTEM            =       0   (CARTESIAN)

INITIAL JOBNAME = file
CURRENT JOBNAME = file
*** ANSYS GLOBAL STATUS ***
```

The model has **879 elements** and **1817 nodes**. Save your work so far.

SOLUTION

14. Main Menu > Solution > Solve > Current LS > OK

POSTPROCESSING

First plot the von Mises element solution to get an idea about the accuracy of the initial mesh. Your meshes/results may differ slightly from those shown.

15. Main Menu > General Postproc > Plot Results > Contour Plot > Element Solu > Stress > von Mises stress > OK

The element solution plot shows discontinuous stress contours across element boundaries indicating poor accuracy for this coarse mesh. The maximum computed value is around 224 N per mm^2 (224 MPa), which is about 9 per cent higher than the value calculated with the axisymmetric model in Lesson 3.

Clearly we will need a finer mesh in order to have confidence in the results. Ordinarily, of course, the answer is not known in advance as in this case, and we must employ previous experience and good judgment to arrive at satisfactory results.

Figure 4-8 Von Mises stress.

Return to the Preprocessor and refine the mesh. It may be necessary to remove the pressures from areas before remeshing. It is **important** to **save your work before remeshing**. The remesh could request more nodes and elements than are available with your license, and ANSYS will **shut down**. (*Skip these steps if your ANSYS license is limited to 16,000 nodes.*) For other options, see **4-5 Smart Sizing** below.

16. Main Menu > Preprocessor > Loads > Define Loads > Delete > Structural > Pressure > On Areas Select the three areas that make up the inside surface. **> OK > OK.**

17. Main Menu > Preprocessor > Meshing > Modify Mesh > Refine at > All > Level of Refinement 1 > OK

After refining the mesh everywhere, refine the area at the fillet on the inside of the cylinder.

18. Main Menu > Preprocessor > Meshing > Modify Mesh > Refine At > Areas (pick the fillet area) **> Level of Refinement   1 > OK**

Figure 4-9 Refined mesh.

A list of the database shows a model with about **17,000 nodes** and **10,000 elements**.

Now it's necessary to reapply the pressure load.

19. Main Menu > Preprocessor > Loads > Define Loads > Apply > Structural > Pressure > On Areas
Select the three areas that make up the inside surface and set **pressure = 35 > OK**

Return to the SOLUTION. The solution may now take a perceptible amount of time depending upon the speed of your computer. Use the Postprocessor to plot the von Mises stress and zoom in on the fillet region.

Figure 4-10 Von Mises stress.

Using the **Results Viewer**, the maximum von Mises stress is found to be about 210 N per mm^2 with this mesh, and while the element solution stress contour plots are not as smooth as one might like, these results are fairly accurate. If we continue with the mesh refinement we would expect to see the stress levels converge to some stable values.

It is also important to check the stresses at points away from the fillet to see how they compare with theoretical values.

Figure 4-11 Node numbering at inner surface.

The node at the inside surface on the left happens to be number 20 again (your numbering scheme may be different). In this location SX corresponds to the radial stress component, SY the axial component, and SZ the hoop component.

Theoretical Solution:

Radial Stress (SX) = -35 N per mm^2

Axial Stress (SY) = 45 N per mm^2

Hoop Stress (SZ) = 125 N per mm^2

ANSYS Solution:

NODE	SX	SY	SZ	SXY	SYZ	SXZ
20	-34.872	46.476	127.48	-0.32668E-01	-0.11214E	-01-0.29094

And the computed results are seen to have good accuracy.

4-5 SMART SIZE

There are a number of parameters and options available in ANSYS for use during mesh creation. One of these is the **smart size** option that employs meshing rules to adjust the element density to the geometry of the model. Either clear the mesh from the model used in the previous tutorial (**Preprocessor > Meshing > Clear > Volumes**) or start the problem again and mesh the volume again. In either case, turn smart size on before creating the initial mesh.

1. Main Menu > Preprocessor > Meshing > Size Cntls > Smart Size > Basic > LVL Size Level > 3 > OK

2. Main Menu > Preprocessor > Meshing > Mesh > Volumes > Free > (pick the solid) **> OK**

This operation creates the mesh with around 800 elements and 1600 nodes shown on the left in the figure below. This mesh has a much better element shape and distribution through the thickness of the vessel than the mesh of Figure 4-5 that was created using the default setting with smart size off.

Figure 4-12 Smart size meshes.

The mesh on the right was obtained from **Modify Mesh > All > LEVEL Level of refinement 1**. It has around 6500 elements and 10700 nodes and produced a maximum von Mises stress comparable to that found with the high-density mesh axisymmetric model.

4-6 CYCLIC SYMMETRY

The 3-D pressure vessel problem can be solved with a much smaller model than those above. With the 90-degree slice, the boundary restraints on exposed faces are conveniently aligned with global coordinate directions X, Y, Z, but we can use a much smaller slice if the displacements normal to the exposed face can be set to zero.

We illustrate the ideas by solving the problem again working with a **15-degree** slice defined in **global cylindrical coordinates**.

4-7 TUTORIAL 4B – USING CYCLIC SYMMETRY

1. Start ANSYS and establish jobname and working directory as usual.

2. Import a 15-degree solid model of the pressure vessel or use ANSYS commands to create the 15-degree wedge. Select the **ten-node tetrahedron**, element number **187**.

3. Utility Menu > WorkPlane > Change Active CS (Coordinate System) to > Global Cylindrical Y

The angular coordinate theta corresponds to a rotation about the Y-axis.

Displacement Boundary conditions are applied to restrain displacement in the **Z direction** on the **X-Y plane (left face)** of the wedge.

4. Main Menu > Preprocessor > Loads > Define Loads > Apply > Structural > Displ > On Areas Select the X-Y face (left side in figure below) and set **UZ = 0.**

On the symmetric face of the wedge apply Symmetric Displacement conditions.

5. Main Menu > Preprocessor > Loads > Define Loads > Apply > Structural > Displacement > Symmetry B.C. > On Areas (Select the symmetric face, right side in figure) **> OK**

The S's in the figure below indicate the symmetric boundary conditions.

Figure 4-13 Applying symmetric boundary conditions.

Restrain the lower surface of the wedge from displacement in the **Y direction (UY = 0)**, and then apply a **pressure** of 35 N per mm^2 to the interior surface. Create the mesh.

6. Main Menu > Preprocessor > Meshing > Size Cntls > Smart Size > Basic > LVL Size Level > 6 (default) **> OK**

7. Main Menu > Preprocessor > Meshing > Mesh > Volumes > Free > (pick the solid) **> OK**

8. Modify Mesh > All > LEVEL Level of refinement 1 > OK

9. Modify Mesh > Areas > (pick fillet area) **LEVEL Level of refinement 1 > OK**

10. Now **solve** and **plot** the element solution von Miscs stress contours. Use Results Viewer. The maximum von Mises stress is about 205 N per mm^2, about the as our best estimate from the axisymmetric model. This mesh contains about 2000 elements and 3700 nodes, around 30 per cent of the size of the 90-degree model and displays better accuracy.

Figure 4-14 Von Mises stresses.

Figure 4-15 Flange.

The approach just described is particularly useful for the analysis of items with **cyclic symmetry** such as the flange shown in the figure above. If the geometry, boundary conditions, loadings, and materials are symmetric with respect to an axis of revolution, we can use a **sector,** say from the center of one hole to the center of the next hole, for analysis and use symmetric boundary conditions when building the model. (Alternatively, you could use a sector centered about a hole.)

4-8 BRICKS

The ANSYS element library also includes **eight-node** and **twenty-node hexahedra** (bricks) for three-dimensional modeling. These elements can collapse into wedge, pyramid, or tetrahedron shaped elements. The straight-sided eight-node elements can be used for simple geometries with straight edges. However, the twenty-node element permits modeling of curved surfaces and provides much greater accuracy than the eight-node element. The twenty-node element is shown in the accompanying figure. It is easy to visualize filling a six-faced region with brick elements, but a completely arbitrarily shaped solid can sometimes be difficult to mesh this way.

Figure 4-16 20-node brick elements.

Mapped Meshes: ANSYS provides a number of meshing methods. With the mapped method, a regular pattern of bricks is mapped onto a six, five or four-faced solid. Examples are shown below.

Figure 4-17 Mapped mesh examples.

To utilize mapped meshing techniques, the solid must have identifiable four, five or six-sided sub-volumes. If these do not exist, they may be created by concatenating areas, adding planes, etc. Since they have fewer elements and nodes, mapped brick meshes solve faster than equivalent tetrahedron meshes, but their creation can often require more engineering time.

Let us return to the pressure vessel to illustrate the mapped meshing process. The basic 90-degree solid has been divided into **three six-sided** and **one five-sided** component solids and those components **glued** together to preserve the boundary planes between them.

Figure 4-18 Vessel solid.

In the next tutorial we mesh and solve this problem using twenty-node brick elements.

4-9 TUTORIAL 4C –MAPPED MESH PRESSURE VESSEL

The geometry is developed by using keypoints and lines to create areas and by sweeping the areas through 90 degrees to form the volumes. The volumes are then glued together.

1. Start ANSYS, etc.

2. Read the following text file of keypoints and lines using **File > Read Input from . . .**

```
/FILNAM,Tutorial4C
/title, Pressure Vessel Geometry Creation for Mapped Mesh

/prep7
! Create geometry
k, 1,  75.,   0.          ! Keypoint 1 is at 75.0, 0.0
k, 2, 100.,   0.
k, 3, 100., 150.
k, 4, 100., 200.
k, 5,  50., 200.
k, 6,   0., 200.
k, 7,   0., 175.
k, 8,  50., 175.
k, 9,  75., 150.
k, 10,  50., 150.

x11 = 50. + 25.*cos(45/57.29578)     ! Coords of k11
y11 = 150. + 25.*sin(45/57.29578)

k, 11, x11, y11

L, 9, 1                   ! Line from keypoints 9 to 1
L, 1, 2
L, 2, 3
L, 3, 4
L, 4, 5
L, 5, 6
L, 6, 7
L, 7, 8
L, 9, 3
L, 8, 5
L, 4, 11

larc, 9, 11, 10, 25.  ! Fillet arc
larc, 11, 8, 10, 25.

al, 1, 2, 3, 9          ! Area defined by lines 1,2,3,9
al, 9, 4, 11, 12
al, 13, 11, 5, 10
al, 8, 10, 6, 7


! rotate all areas about k6-k7 axis through 90 deg.
```

```
vrotat, all, , , , , , 6, 7, 90.
! glue all volumes together

vglue,all
```

For more information on these commands, search the ANSYS help file. The geometry created by this text file is shown below. (Alternatively use your CAD system to manipulate the geometry.)

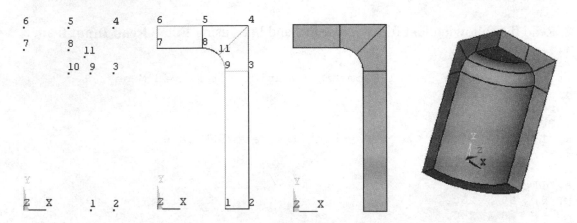

Figure 4-19 Pressure vessel keypoints, lines, areas, and volumes.

Select the twenty-node brick element.

3. Main Menu > Preprocessor > Element Type > Add/Edit/Delete > Add > Solid > Brick 20 node186 > OK

4. Enter material properties **EX = 2.0E5** and **PRXY = 0.3** as before.

Mesh each of the four volumes separately. Use size controls to specify the number of elements along each edge; 2 through the wall thickness, 10 over the 0 to 90 degree arc, and 4 along the remaining edge. Start with the large lower volume.

Figure 4-20 Edge divisions.

5. Main Menu > Preprocessor > Meshing > Size Cntrls > Manual Size > Lines > Picked Lines > (pick the wall thickness dimension) **> OK Enter NDIV No. element divisions = 2 > OK** (KYNDIV SIZE,NDIV can be changed to **no** if need be.)

Figure 4-21 Element sizes on picked lines.

6. Repeat step 5 for the other two edges giving them 4 and 10 divisions each.

Then complete the mapping for this component.

7. Main Menu > Preprocessor > Meshing > Mesh > Volumes > Mapped > 4 to 6 sided. Pick the lower solid component. The mesh shown on the left below is created.

8. Repeat step 5 for the two circular arc edges of the fillet.

Only a minimum number of edge division definitions need to be made; compatibility along glued boundary edges will be enforced during the meshing operation.

Figure 4-22 Mapped meshes.

9. Repeat the meshing process for the other three solid components. The mesh on the above right is developed.

10. Apply displacement boundary conditions and pressures as before and Solve.

This model has about 390 elements and 2366 nodes and is solved in a few seconds. The maximum von Mises stress is around 11 per cent lower than our best estimate from the axisymmetric solution, so we need a higher density mesh in several regions to obtain better accuracy.

Figure 4-23 Von Mises stress contours.

4-10 SWEEPING

Three-dimensional meshes can also be created for volumes by sweeping a two-dimensional mesh along or about a line. One must select a 2-D element for the area and a 3-D element for the volume. The 2-D mesh is temporary and can be automatically eliminated after the solid mesh is created. To illustrate, consider the pressure vessel one last time.

4-11 TUTORIAL 4D – SWEPT MESH

1. Create the volumes as in Tutorial 4C.

Select the 8-node quad element to mesh the area and the 20-node brick for the volume.

2. Main Menu > Preprocessor > Element Type > Add/Edit/Delete > Add > Solid > Quad 8 node 183 > OK

3. Main Menu > Preprocessor > Element Type > Add/Edit/Delete > Add > Solid > Brick 20 node 186 > OK

We will create a mapped 2-D mesh on the lower part of the solid. Use size controls to specify **three** elements through the thickness and **six** elements along the height direction.

4. Main Menu > Preprocessor > Meshing > Size Cntrls > Manual Size > Lines > Picked Lines > (pick the wall thickness dimension *in the X-Y plane*.) > OK. Enter 3 for NDIV No. element divisions > OK

5. Do the same for the height with NDIV = 6

6. Main Menu > Preprocessor > Meshing > Mesh > Areas > Mapped > 3 to 4 sided
Pick the area on the left vertical edge of the solid. The quad mesh below is created.

Figure 4-24 Quad mesh on lower edge.

7. Utility Menu > Plot > Volumes (To show the solid again.)

8. Main Menu > Preprocessor > Meshing > Mesh > Volume Sweep > Sweep Opts
Select the options shown below.

Sweep Options	✕

[EXTOPT] Set extrusion options used by VSWEEP

☑ Clear area elements after sweeping

☐ Tet mesh in nonsweepable volumes

☐ Auto select source and target areas

Number of divisions in sweep direction   10

Spacing ratio in sweep direction   0

| OK | Cancel | Help |

Figure 4-25 Sweep options.

9. Main Menu > Preprocessor > Meshing > Mesh > Volume Sweep > Sweep

Pick volume to be swept (Select lower portion of vessel) > **OK**

Pick source area (Select the area we just meshed with quads)
> **OK** (Watch the message window lower left.)

Pick target area (Select the area on the right side at 90 deg
rotation) > **OK**

This process can be repeated to develop the remainder of the
pressure vessel mesh. The sweep can also be performed along
a line, and we can use triangular 2-D elements if a wedge type
of solid element is desired.

Figure 4-26 Swept mesh.

4-12 SUMMARY

This lesson concentrated on problem formulation, mesh development, solution, and
results evaluation of three-dimensional problems. Free-tetrahedron, mapped-brick, and
swept-brick or wedge meshes were developed and employed in the solution of the
pressure vessel problem introduced in Lesson 3. Solution and post processing these kinds
of problems was also illustrated.

To speed up the solution of large problems, you may want to select a working directory
on your local workstation to avoid network data transfers during solution. Also
investigate alternate solution methods. **Solution > Analysis Type > Sol'n Controls >
Sol'n Options.**

Many 3-D problems do not have planes of symmetry and must be considered in their entirety. An example of such a part is shown below.

Figure 4-27 Lever model.

The part in the preceding figure is also an example where one might want to use a combined mesh of brick and tetrahedron elements. It might be desirable to map mesh the cylindrical component with bricks and the remaining portion with tets and wedges.

4-13 PROBLEMS

Use 3-D modeling methods to solve the following problems from Lesson 2:

4-1 Problem 2-1

4-2 Problem 2-2

4-3 Problem 2-3

4-4 Problem 2-4

4-5 Problem 2-5

4-6 Problem 2-6

4-7 Problem 2-7

4-8 The lever arm of Figure 4-27 is restrained in all DOF on the interior surface of the cylindrical bore and has a vertical load on the short segment of the 'L' shaped surface. Apply the total load as a series of equal concentrated forces on the nodes of the short segment. The over all length is 5 inches and the bore ID is 0.75 inches. Otherwise, select your own dimensions, materials and loads. Determine the values and location of the maximum deflection and the maximum stresses. Is failure likely to occur if the material is a ductile steel? A brittle cast iron?

4-9 Use tetrahedron solid modeling methods to solve the stress concentration problem of Lesson 2, Tutorial 2A. The model can be brought in as an IGES file, or you can use ANSYS geometry building commands to extrude an area to form a solid. Compare the results with those from Tutorial 2A and comment upon the relative ease and effectiveness of each approach.

4-10 Same as 4-9 but use 8-node bricks, then twenty-node bricks.

Lesson 5

Beams

5-1 OVERVIEW

Lesson 5 treats problems in structural analysis where the most suitable modeling choice is a **beam** element. Like the truss and the plate, the beam is a structural element, and like the truss element it is a **line element**. Its formulation is based upon the engineering study of the behavior of beams as practical structural members. The lesson discusses

   ♦ Creating text file FEM beam models.

   ♦ Modeling 2-D and 3-D problems and evaluating the results.

5-2 INTRODUCTION

When long, slender bars are subjected to planar moments they bend in such as way that maximum compression is produced at one extreme surface and maximum tension at the other. Somewhere in between the strain is zero, and the strains and stresses vary linearly from this **neutral axis**. Such behavior is an example of pure bending.

Figure 5-1 Beam bending by moments.

The situation is not much different when transverse forces cause bending, and we can determine the state of deformation by keeping track of the **displacement** of the neutral axis and its **slope**. Thus in finite element modeling of beams, we need to utilize slope variables in addition to the displacement variables used in previous lessons.

Figure 5-2 shows a simply supported structure composed of three beam elements carrying a point force, a concentrated moment and a distributed load. The deflected shape, displacement variables, and slope variables are also shown.

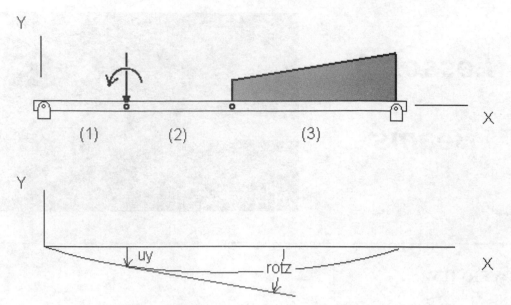

Figure 5-2 Three-element model of beam.

ANSYS provides the engineer with an elastic beam element called **BEAM3** for two-dimensional modeling. The flexural inertia of the beam cross section provides stiffness to resist bending loadings, and its cross sectional area gives it stiffness to resist axial loads just like a truss element does.

5-3 TUTORIAL 5A – CANTILEVER BEAM

Objective: Determine the end deflection and root bending stress of a steel cantilever beam modeled as a 2-D problem.

The ANSYS 2-D beam element '**beam3**' is used for modeling. The ten-inch long beam is represented by ten beam3 elements connecting 11 nodes along the global X-axis. Cantilever boundary conditions at the left end prevent axial (UX), vertical (UY) and rotation about the z axis (ROTZ) deformations.

Figure 5-3 Cantilever beam.

Figure 5-4 Ten-element model.

The problem is formulated using a text file incorporating a **consistent set of units**, pounds force and inches in this case. The computed results will have deflections in inches, slopes in radians, shear forces in pounds, moments in inch-pounds, and stresses in psi.

```
/FILNAM,Tutorial5A
/title, 10 Element,2D Cantilever Beam
/prep7
!List of Nodes
n,  1,  0.0,  0.0      ! Node 1 is located at (0.0, 0.0) inches
n,  2,  1.0,  0.0
n,  3,  2.0,  0.0
n,  4,  3.0,  0.0
n,  5,  4.0,  0.0
n,  6,  5.0,  0.0
n,  7,  6.0,  0.0
n,  8,  7.0,  0.0
n,  9,  8.0,  0.0
n, 10,  9.0,  0.0
n, 11, 10.0,  0.0

et, 1, beam3           ! Element type; no.1 is beam3

!Material Properties
mp, ex, 1, 3.e7        ! Elastic modulus for material number 1 in psi
mp, prxy, 1, 0.3       ! Poisson's ratio

! Real constant set 1 for a 0.5 x 0.375 rectangular xsctn beam.
! Area, Izz (flexural Inertia), height 'h' as in sigma = Mc/I, c = h/2
! A = 0.1875 sq.in., Izz = 0.0022 in^4, h = 0.375 inch

r, 1, 0.1875, 0.0022, 0.375

!List of elements and nodes they connect
en,  1,  1,  2         ! Element Number 1 connects nodes 1 & 2
en,  2,  2,  3
en,  3,  3,  4
en,  4,  4,  5
en,  5,  5,  6
en,  6,  6,  7
en,  7,  7,  8
en,  8,  8,  9
en,  9,  9, 10
en, 10, 10, 11
```

```
!Displacement Boundary Conditions
d, 1, ux, 0.0           ! Displacement at node 1 in x-dir is zero
d, 1, uy, 0.0           ! Displacement at node 1 in y-dir is zero
d, 1, rotz, 0.0         ! Rotation about z axis at node 1 is zero

!Applied Force
f, 11, fy, -50.    ! Force at node 11 in negative y-direction is 50 lbf.

/pnum, elem, 1          ! Plot element numbers
eplot                   ! Plot the elements
finish

/solu                   ! Select static load solution
antype, static
solve
finish

/post1
```

1. Start ANSYS, etc., read the input file using **File > Read Input from . . .**

Plot the deformed shape and examine the **computed deflections** and **slopes**.

2. Main Menu > General Postproc > List Results > Nodal Solution > DOF Solution > Y-Component of displacement > OK

```
PRINT U     NODAL SOLUTION PER NODE

  ***** POST1 NODAL DEGREE OF FREEDOM LISTING *****

 LOAD STEP=      1  SUBSTEP=       1
  TIME=     1.0000      LOAD CASE=   0

 THE FOLLOWING DEGREE OF FREEDOM RESULTS ARE IN THE GLOBAL COORDINATE
SYSTEM

    NODE      UY
       1   0.0000
       2  -0.36616E-02
       3  -0.14141E-01
       4  -0.30682E-01
       5  -0.52525E-01
       6  -0.78914E-01
       7  -0.10909
       8  -0.14230
       9  -0.17778
      10  -0.21477
      11  -0.25253

 MAXIMUM ABSOLUTE VALUES
 NODE           11
 VALUE  -0.25253
```

3. Main Menu > General Postproc > List Results > Nodal Solution > DOF Solution > Y-Component of displacement > OK

```
PRINT ROT   NODAL SOLUTION PER NODE

  ***** POST1 NODAL DEGREE OF FREEDOM LISTING *****

  LOAD STEP=     1  SUBSTEP=      1
   TIME=     1.0000      LOAD CASE=    0

  THE FOLLOWING DEGREE OF FREEDOM RESULTS ARE IN THE GLOBAL COORDINATE
SYSTEM

     NODE      ROTZ
        1    0.0000
        2   -0.71970E-02
        3   -0.13636E-01
        4   -0.19318E-01
        5   -0.24242E-01
        6   -0.28409E-01
        7   -0.31818E-01
        8   -0.34470E-01
        9   -0.36364E-01
       10   -0.37500E-01
       11   -0.37879E-01

 MAXIMUM ABSOLUTE VALUES
 NODE            11
 VALUE   -0.37879E-01
```

The **maximum deflection UY and slope ROTZ** occur at node 11 at the free end as expected.

The maximum values –0.25253 inch and –0.037879 radian agree with results you can calculate from solid mechanics beam theory. Confirm these results with a simple hand calculation. To examine the **computed bending stress**:

4. Main Menu > General Postproc > List Results > Element Solution > Line Elements Results > Element Results > OK

```
PRINT ELEM ELEMENT SOLUTION PER ELEMENT

 ***** POST1 ELEMENT SOLUTION LISTING *****

  LOAD STEP     1  SUBSTEP=     1
   TIME=     1.0000      LOAD CASE=   0

EL=      1 NODES=       1       2  MAT=   1
BEAM3
 TEMP =    0.00     0.00     0.00     0.00
 LOCATION   SDIR        SBYT         SBYB
  1 (I)    0.0000      42614.      -42614.
  2 (J)    0.0000      38352.      -38352.
```

```
LOCATION   SMAX        SMIN
 1 (I)     42614.      -42614.
 2 (J)     38352.      -38352.
LOCATION   EPELDIR     EPELBYT      EPELBYB
 1 (I)     0.000000    0.001420    -0.001420
 2 (J)     0.000000    0.001278    -0.001278
LOCATION   EPTHDIR     EPTHBYT      EPTHBYB
 1 (I)     0.000000    0.000000     0.000000
 2 (J)     0.000000    0.000000     0.000000
EPINAXL =      0.000000


EL=       2  NODES=        2       3  MAT=   1
BEAM3
 TEMP =    0.00     0.00     0.00    0.00
LOCATION   SDIR        SBYT         SBYB
 1 (I)     0.0000      38352.      -38352.
 2 (J)     0.0000      34091.      -34091.
LOCATION   SMAX        SMIN
 1 (I)     38352.      -38352.
 2 (J)     34091.      -34091.
LOCATION   EPELDIR     EPELBYT      EPELBYB
 1 (I)     0.000000    0.001278    -0.001278
 2 (J)     0.000000    0.001136    -0.001136
LOCATION   EPTHDIR     EPTHBYT      EPTHBYB
 1 (I)     0.000000    0.000000     0.000000
 2 (J)     0.000000    0.000000     0.000000
EPINAXL =      0.000000
```

The stresses in each beam element are given in the form shown. **SDIR** is the direct or **axial stress** and **SBYT** and **SBYB** are the bending stresses (top and bottom). **SBYT** and **SBYB** are equal for a symmetric cross section beam. **SMAX = SDIR + SBYT** and **SMIN = SDIR - SBYT**; the sum and difference of the direct and bending stress components. SDIR is zero in this example because there is no applied axial force. All quantities are given at each end of the element; that is, at the first named node I and at the second named node J. (Note: if the section is not symmetric, let h = twice the distance from the neutral axis to the location where you want the bending stress.)

The **maximum bending stress** of 42,614 psi occurs in beam element 1 at the support, and the value agrees with what you would compute using elementary beam theory, Mc/I.

The displacement and stress solution for this problem is solved just as accurately with **ONE 10-inch long element** connecting nodes at each end of the beam. The deformed shape plot however would show a straight line connecting the two nodes because the plotting software does not use computed slope information. If examining the deformed shape is important or if the spatial mass distribution needs to be accurately represented, use several nodes along the length as described above, otherwise two nodes will do the job, but the plotted results may look funny.

Axial stiffness is included in the beam3 element formulation, so we could add an axial force to the above problem and compute the axial stress and deformation as well. Note however that in the **linear approach** discussed here, the **axial and bending**

deformations are uncoupled. That is, the presence of an axial stress does not influence the bending stiffness. If the bending deformation is small, this approach is usually completely satisfactory.

Figure 5-5 Transverse and axial loads.

To illustrate this, add an axial force of 1000 lbf to the end of the beam and solve the problem again.

Add this line to the text file   **f, 11, fx, 1000**

5. Utility Menu > File > Clear & Start new > OK > Yes

6. Utility Menu > File > Read Input from . . . (read in the file with the axial load added.)

List the displacements.

7. Main Menu > General Postproc > List Results > Nodal Solution > DOF Solution > Displacement vector sum > OK

```
***** POST1 NODAL DEGREE OF FREEDOM LISTING *****

LOAD STEP=      1  SUBSTEP=      1
 TIME=     1.0000      LOAD CASE=   0

THE FOLLOWING DEGREE OF FREEDOM RESULTS ARE IN GLOBAL COORDINATES

    NODE      UX            UY            UZ            USUM
       1  0.0000        0.0000        0.0000        0.0000
       2  0.17778E-03  -0.36616E-02   0.0000        0.36659E-02
       3  0.35556E-03  -0.14141E-01   0.0000        0.14146E-01
       4  0.53333E-03  -0.30682E-01   0.0000        0.30686E-01
       5  0.71111E-03  -0.52525E-01   0.0000        0.52530E-01
       6  0.88889E-03  -0.78914E-01   0.0000        0.78919E-01
       7  0.10667E-02  -0.10909       0.0000        0.10910
       8  0.12444E-02  -0.14230       0.0000        0.14230
       9  0.14222E-02  -0.17778       0.0000        0.17778
      10  0.16000E-02  -0.21477       0.0000        0.21478
      11  0.17778E-02  -0.25253       0.0000        0.25253

MAXIMUM ABSOLUTE VALUES
NODE          11            11            0            11
VALUE    0.17778E-02-0.25253      0.0000        0.25253
```

The deflections show axial deformations now, but the bending displacements and slopes are exactly the same as before indicating no interaction between the axial and bending loads.

List the stresses. (Results for the first element are shown.)

8. Main Menu > General Postproc > List Results > Element Solution > Line Element Results > Element Results > OK

```
PRINT ELEM ELEMENT SOLUTION PER ELEMENT

 ***** POST1 ELEMENT SOLUTION LISTING *****

   LOAD STEP     1   SUBSTEP=       1
   TIME=    1.0000           LOAD CASE=   0


 EL=       1   NODES=         1        2   MAT=  1
BEAM3
 TEMP =     0.00     0.00     0.00     0.00
 LOCATION    SDIR        SBYT        SBYB
   1 (I)    5333.3      42614.      -42614.
   2 (J)    5333.3      38352.      -38352.
 LOCATION    SMAX        SMIN
   1 (I)    47947.     -37280.
   2 (J)    43686.     -33019.
 LOCATION   EPELDIR     EPELBYT      EPELBYB
   1 (I)    0.000178    0.001420    -0.001420
   2 (J)    0.000178    0.001278    -0.001278
 LOCATION   EPTHDIR     EPTHBYT      EPTHBYB
   1 (I)    0.000000    0.000000     0.000000
   2 (J)    0.000000    0.000000     0.000000
 EPINAXL =      0.000000
```

The added axial load produces a direct tensile stress (P/A) of 5333 psi that is combined with the bending stresses to give maximum and minimum values of 47,947 psi on the top of the beam and –37,280 psi on the bottom at node 1.

For problems with **large deformations**, the nonlinear coupling of axial stress and bending stiffness must be considered and ANSYS **nonlinear solution** options employed. What is large and what is small for a given problem? Some previous experience and/or numerical experimentation can help answer that question.

5-4 2-D FRAME

As another example of beam element modeling with ANSYS, we find the stress and deflection distribution in the two-dimensional frame of Figure 5-6. This model is contrived to include most of the possible situations one might encounter, including a downward force (**7000 lbf**), a concentrated moment (**1000 in-lbf**) and a wind load acting on the left side. The wind loading is developed from the load per area acting on the side of the structure that is converted to a line loading in load per unit length. It varies from **10 lbf/in** at the top to **zero lbf/in** at the bottom.

Figure 5-6 Frame.

The frame is constructed of **W8x10** standard shape beams. The area of the cross section is **2.96 sq. in.** and the flexural inertia is **30.8 in**^{4}. The total section depth is **7.89 in**. The frame is rigidly attached at its left support but allowed to pivot at its right support. If the I beams are made of A36 steel (Sy = 36,000 psi), will any yielding occur?

5-5 TUTORIAL 5B – 2-D FRAME

We use a text file to define the model, and perform the solution and postprocessing interactively. Note that the node dimensions are converted from feet to inches in the text file.

1. Start ANSYS and enter the following data using **Read Input From …** Then **Plot > Elements**, etc.

```
/FILNAM,Tutorial5B
/title, Tutorial 5B – 2-D Frame

/prep7

et, 1, beam3    ! Element type; no.1 is beam3

!Material Properties
mp, ex, 1, 3.e7          ! Elastic modulus
mp, prxy, 1, 0.3         ! Poisson's ratio
mp, dens, 1, 0.283/386.  ! Mass density
```

Figure 5-7 Frame model.

```
!List of Nodes
n,  1,  0.0,       0.0       ! Node 1 is located at (0.0, 0.0)inches
! Convert from feet to inches for consistent units.
n,  2, 10.0*12,  0.0
n,  3,  0.0,      12.0*12
n,  4,  5.0*12,   12.0*12
n,  5, 10.0*12,   12.0*12
n,  6,  0.0,      24.0*12
n,  7, 10.0*12,   24.0*12


! Real constant set 1 for W8x10 I beam.
! Area, Izz (flexural Inertia), height 'h' as in sigma = Mc/I, c = h/2
! A = 2.96 sq.in., Izz = 30.8 in^4, h = 7.89 inch

r, 1, 2.96, 30.8, 7.89

!List of elements and nodes they connect
en,  1,  1,  3          ! Element Number 1 connects nodes 1 & 3
en,  2,  2,  5
en,  3,  3,  4
en,  4,  4,  5
en,  5,  3,  6
en,  6,  5,  7
en,  7,  6,  7


!Displacement Boundary Conditions
d, 1, ux, 0.0         ! Displacement at node 1 in x-dir is zero
d, 1, uy, 0.0         ! Displacement at node 1 in y-dir is zero
d, 1, rotz, 0.0       ! Rotation about z axis at node 1 is zero

d, 2, ux, 0.0
d, 2, uy, 0.0

!Applied Loadings
f, 4, fy, -7000. ! Force at node 4 in negative y-direction is 7000 lbf.
f, 4, mz, -1000  ! Moment about Z axis is -1000 in-lbf

sfbeam, 1, 1, pres, 0, 5    ! Surface Force on beam 1 varies from 0 to 5
sfbeam, 5, 1, pres, 5, 10

acel, 0, 386., 0      ! acceleration of gravity for weight loading

finish
```

Note that boundary conditions must be supplied for the slope variables and that here line loads are applied to the beam elements using the **sfbeam** command. Each beam element has a local coordinate axis with local *x* directed from **node I** (first named node) to **node J** (second named node) and with *y* and *z* axes according to the right hand rule with *z* directed toward the viewer. The direction of the surface loading requires some pre-analysis planning and/or interactive experimentation with the model to get things right. To view the loads and element coordinate systems.

2. Utility Menu > PlotCtrls > Symbols > [/PSF] Surface Load Symbols (set to **Pressures**) and **Show pres and convect as** (set to **Arrows**).

Utility Menu > PlotCtrls > Symbols > ESYS Element Coordinate sys (set to **ON**).

To view the concentrated moment and the slope boundary condition, select **ISO** in the **Pan, Zoom, Rotate** options.

3. Main Menu > Solution > Solve > Current LS > OK

When plotting the deformed shape, notice that even though the beam element deformed shape has been correctly computed, as a plotting convenience the nodes are connected by straight lines. If you want to visualize the beam element shape, include a few extra nodes and elements between the points of the beam connections.

Figure 5-8 Deformed frame.

4. Main Menu > General Postprocess > Plot Results > Deformed Shape > Def + undeformed.

Now list the nodal deflection values.

5. Main Menu > General Postproc > List Results > Nodal Solution > DOF Solution > Displacement vector sum > OK

```
PRINT DOF   NODAL SOLUTION PER NODE

 ***** POST1 NODAL DEGREE OF FREEDOM LISTING *****

 LOAD STEP=      1  SUBSTEP=      1
  TIME=     1.0000     LOAD CASE=   0

 THE FOLLOWING DEGREE OF FREEDOM RESULTS ARE IN GLOBAL COORDINATES

     NODE       UX            UY            UZ          USUM
        1     0.0000        0.0000        0.0000       0.0000
        2     0.0000        0.0000        0.0000       0.0000
        3     0.49528      -0.35297E-02   0.0000       0.49529
        4     0.49537      -0.14501       0.0000       0.51616
        5     0.49547      -0.87344E-02   0.0000       0.49555
        6     0.73410      -0.31099E-02   0.0000       0.73411
        7     0.73316      -0.95128E-02   0.0000       0.73322

 MAXIMUM ABSOLUTE VALUES
 NODE          6             4             0            6
 VALUE      0.73410      -0.14501       0.0000       0.73411
```

As an alternative to the method used in the Tutorial 5A to examine stress results, here we will create an Element Table. Because the direct and bending stresses combine to produce different results on the top and bottom of the beam and also produce different results at each end of the beam, we will create four element table entries using interactive commands.

6. Main Menu > General Postprocess > Element Table > Define Table > Add

Enter a label you choose such as **SmaxI** and scroll down to find **By sequence num**.

Select **NMISC** and enter **1** (to the right of NMISC) > **Apply**.

Figure 5-9 Define element table quantities.

Repeat for

Label **SminI, By sequence num**, **NMISC, 2 > Apply**

Label **SmaxJ, By sequence num**, **NMISC, 3 > Apply**

Label **SminJ, By sequence num**, **NMISC, 4 > OK > Close Element Table Data**

This sets up tabular data for Smax and Smin at nodes I and J for each element.

7. Main Menu > General Postprocess > Element Table > List Elem Table (Click on the first four items SMAXI, SMINI, etc.) > **OK**

```
┌─────────────────────────────────────────────────────────────┐
│ ⋀ List Element Table Data                              [×]    │
│                                                               │
│  [PRETAB] List Element Table Data                             │
│                                                               │
│  Lab1-9  Items to be listed          ┌──────────────────┐▲    │
│                                       │NMIS1             │▒    │
│                                       │NMIS2             │▒    │
│                                       │NMIS3             │▒    │
│                                       │NMIS4             │▒    │
│                                       │Items  1-10 GRP1  │     │
│                                       │Items 11-20 GRP2  │▼    │
│                                       └──────────────────┘     │
│                                                               │
│                                                               │
│    ┌────────┐   ┌────────┐   ┌────────┐   ┌────────┐         │
│    │   OK   │   │ Apply  │   │ Cancel │   │  Help  │         │
│    └────────┘   └────────┘   └────────┘   └────────┘         │
└─────────────────────────────────────────────────────────────┘
```

Figure 5-10 Table data to list.

The resulting element stresses are shown in the table below.

```
PRINT ELEMENT TABLE ITEMS PER ELEMENT

  ***** POST1 ELEMENT TABLE LISTING *****

    STAT    CURRENT     CURRENT     CURRENT     CURRENT
    ELEM     SMAXI       SMINI       SMAXJ       SMINJ
      1     10119.     -11631.      2525.3     -3955.3
      2    -1840.0     -1840.0      8431.5    -12030.
      3      515.64     -419.78    18113.     -18017.
      4    18241.     -18145.      18439.     -18343.
      5     2839.7     -2705.5      1099.5      -883.83
      6     7978.0     -8343.0      4545.1     -4828.7
      7      756.35    -1227.0      4451.6     -4922.2

MINIMUM VALUES
ELEM           2           4           5           4
VALUE    -1840.0     -18145.      1099.5     -18343.

MAXIMUM VALUES
ELEM           4           3           4           5
VALUE    18241.      -419.78    18439.       -883.83
```

A maximum stress of 18,439 psi occurs in element 4, but there will be no yielding in the frame for the material yield stress is 36 kpsi.

You can also plot each of these table data items for a visual indication of the stress distribution in the frame. See below.

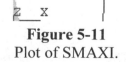

Figure 5-11
Plot of SMAXI.

8. Main Menu > General Postprocess > Element Table > Plot Elem Table (Select the one to plot.) **> OK**

5-6 BEAM MODELS IN 3-D

When a beam element is incorporated in a 3-dimensional model, the full 3-D flexibility of the beam must be considered. It can have **axial deformation**, **torsional deformation**, and **bending deformations** in **two principal bending planes.** Each beam of the model must be positioned in space to reflect the proper orientation of the element cross section.

Figure 5-12 Beam DOF.

The correct orientation can be defined by specifying the angular rotation of the element about its longitudinal axis or by employing three node points to define a principal plane of bending for the element. The next tutorial uses the approach with 3 nodes.

5-7 TUTORIAL 5C – 'L' BEAM

Objective: Find the stresses and deflections of a simple 'L'-shaped aluminum beam with one end cantilevered and a point load at the other end.

Figure 5-13 'L'-shaped beam.

The ANSYS 3D beam element **BEAM4** is used in modeling this problem. A typical element located in a **global coordinate system XYZ** is shown below. It connects two nodes **I** and **J,** and has its **local** or **element x-axis** defined by these two nodes. The **local y** and **z** axes are aligned with the principal cross section flexural inertia planes.

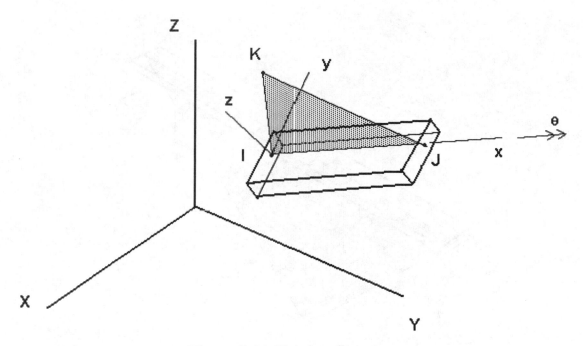

Figure 5-14 Global and local axes.

A third node, **K,** is used to define the **local x-z plane** which is one of the principal planes of bending of the beam. Node K can be another node in the model or a dummy node (with all DOF set to zero) that is used just for orientation purposes. The beam cross sectional properties are defined using an ANSYS 'Real Constants' set. The values for **Izz** and **Iyy** entered into the program **must correspond** to the orientation specified by the three nodes. Check your work carefully. It's easy to get Izz and Iyy reversed.

The Global axis (X,Y,Z) and local axis (x,y,z) definitions for the two elements of the simple problem of this tutorial are illustrated below

Figure 5-15 Orientation of element 1; I = node 1, J = node 2, K = node 3.

Figure 5-16 Orientation of element 2; I = node 2, J = node 3, K = node 1.

Important: The geometric property constant **Ixx** is the **torsional stiffness constant** for the cross section. For circular sections Ixx is equal to the polar moment of inertia (Iyy + Izz). For non-circular sections the torsional stiffness constant is **not** equal to the polar moment of inertia (see torsion of non-circular section in a solid mechanics reference). If no value is entered for Ixx, however, ANSYS will compute the torsional stiffness constant as Iyy + Izz which is correct for circular sections but not correct for non-circular sections.

The text file below defines the simple 'L' – Beam ANSYS model.

```
/FILNAM,Tutorial5C
/title, 3D Beam Sample Problem – An 'L' - Beam
/prep7

n, 1,   0.0,   0.0,   0.0    ! Node 1 is located at (X=0.0, Y=0.0, Z=0.0)
n, 2,   0.0,   0.0,  12.0
n, 3,   6.0,   0.0,  12.0

et, 1, beam4                 ! Element type; no.1 is 3D beam

!Material Properties
mp, ex, 1, 1.e7              ! Elastic modulus, psi
mp, prxy, 1, 0.3            ! Poisson's ratio

! Real properties for beam with 0.25 x 1.0 cross section
! (6 values on first line. 'rmore' for additional values.)

! "r", Set number, Area, Izz, Iyy, thick-z,thick-y,theta,
r, 1, 0.25, 0.001302, 0.0208, 1.0, 0.25, 0

! "rmore", intl strain, Ixx,shear-z,shear-y,spin,addmass
rmore, 0, .004388, , , ,

! element connection and orientation
en, 1, 1, 2, 3      ! Element #1 connects nodes 1 & 2, and
                    ! uses node 3 to define the element local x-z plane.

en, 2, 2, 3, 1      ! Element #2 connects nodes 2 & 3, and
                    ! uses node 1 to define the element local x-z plane.

! Displacement boundary conditions
d, 1, ux, 0.                ! Displacement at node 1 in x-dir is zero
d, 1, uy, 0.
d, 1, uz, 0.
d, 1, rotx, 0.              ! Rotation at node 1 about x-axis is zero
d, 1, roty, 0.
d, 1, rotz, 0.

! (We could have used d, 1, all, 0.0 to define all root restraints.)

! Applied force
f, 3, fy, -5.0              ! Force at node 3 in the negative y-direction
finish

/solu                      ! Select static load solution
antype, static
solve
save
finish

/post1
```

1. Read the problem definition file into ANSYS, and once it's solved, plot the deformed shape.

The deformed plus undeformed beam is shown in the figure below. Nodes were only used at the ends of the 'L' segments so the deformed shape shows a straight-line connection between nodes. The calculated deformations are correct however. You can check the results by hand using the superposition or energy methods.

Figure 5-17 Deformed two-element beam.

The rotation boundary conditions **ROTX, ROTY, ROTZ** are indicated by double-headed arrows, positive by the right-hand rule. They overlay the displacement conditions **UX, UY, UZ** at the cantilever support; on screen the two conditions are shown in different colors. Now list the deflection, slope and stress results.

2. Main Menu > General Postproc > List Results > Nodal Solution > DOF Solution > Displacement vector sum > OK

```
PRINT U    NODAL SOLUTION PER NODE

 ***** POST1 NODAL DEGREE OF FREEDOM LISTING *****

 LOAD STEP=      1  SUBSTEP=      1
  TIME=    1.0000      LOAD CASE=    0

 THE FOLLOWING DEGREE OF FREEDOM RESULTS ARE IN GLOBAL COORDINATES

    NODE      UX           UY           UZ           USUM
       1    0.0000       0.0000       0.0000       0.0000
       2    0.0000      -0.22120      0.0000       0.22120
       3    0.0000      -0.37683      0.0000       0.37683

 MAXIMUM ABSOLUTE VALUES
 NODE           0            3            0            3
 VALUE    0.0000      -0.37683      0.0000       0.37683
```

3. Main Menu > General Postproc > List Results > Nodal Solution > DOF Solution > Displacement vector sum > OK

```
PRINT ROT  NODAL SOLUTION PER NODE

 ***** POST1 NODAL DEGREE OF FREEDOM LISTING *****

 LOAD STEP=      0  SUBSTEP=      1
  TIME=    1.0000      LOAD CASE=   0

 THE FOLLOWING DEGREE OF FREEDOM RESULTS ARE IN THE GLOBAL COORDINATE SYSTEM

     NODE      ROTX        ROTY        ROTZ        RSUM
        1    0.0000      0.0000      0.0000      0.0000
        2    0.27650E-01 0.0000     -0.21331E-01 0.34922E-01
        3    0.27650E-01 0.0000     -0.28243E-01 0.39525E-01

 MAXIMUM ABSOLUTE VALUES
 NODE        2           0           3           3
 VALUE   0.27650E-01  0.0000     -0.28243E-01 0.39525E-01
```

4. Main Menu > General Postproc > List Results > Element Solution > Linie Element Results > Element Results > OK

```
PRINT ELEM ELEMENT SOLUTION PER ELEMENT

 ***** POST1 ELEMENT SOLUTION LISTING *****

  LOAD STEP     1  SUBSTEP=      1
   TIME=    1.0000         LOAD CASE=   0

EL=       1 NODES=       1      2      3 MAT=  1                           BEAM4
TEMP =    0.00     0.00     0.00      0.00    0.00    0.00    0.00    0.00
LOCATION   SDIR        SBYT        SBYB        SBZT        SBZB
   1 (I)   0.0000     -5760.4       5760.4     0.0000      0.0000
   2 (J)   0.0000      0.0000       0.0000     0.0000      0.0000
LOCATION   SMAX        SMIN
   1 (I)   5760.4     -5760.4
   2 (J)   0.0000      0.0000
LOCATION   EPELDIR     EPELBYT     EPELBYB     EPELBZT     EPELBZB
   1 (I)   0.000000   -0.000576    0.000576    0.000000    0.000000
   2 (J)   0.000000    0.000000    0.000000    0.000000    0.000000
LOCATION   EPTHDIR     EPTHBYT     EPTHBYB     EPTHBZT     EPTHBZB
   1 (I)   0.000000    0.000000    0.000000    0.000000    0.000000
   2 (J)   0.000000    0.000000    0.000000    0.000000    0.000000
EPINAXL =     0.000000

EL=       2 NODES=       2      3      1 MAT=  1                           BEAM4
TEMP =    0.00     0.00     0.00      0.00    0.00    0.00    0.00    0.00
LOCATION   SDIR        SBYT         SBYB        SBZT        SBZB
   1 (I)   0.0000     -2880.2        2880.2     0.0000      0.0000
   2 (J)   0.0000     -0.54573E-11 0.54573E-11 0.0000      0.0000
LOCATION   SMAX        SMIN
   1 (I)   2880.2     -2880.2
   2 (J)   0.54573E-11-0.54573E-11
LOCATION   EPELDIR     EPELBYT     EPELBYB     EPELBZT     EPELBZB
   1 (I)   0.000000   -0.000288    0.000288    0.000000    0.000000
   2 (J)   0.000000    0.000000    0.000000    0.000000    0.000000
LOCATION   EPTHDIR     EPTHBYT     EPTHBYB     EPTHBZT     EPTHBZB
   1 (I)   0.000000    0.000000    0.000000    0.000000    0.000000
   2 (J)   0.000000    0.000000    0.000000    0.000000    0.000000
EPINAXL =     0.000000
```

These stress values can be checked easily by hand since the simple 'L'-beam is statically determinate. (SBYT = the bending stress on the +y local axis side of the beam.) An element table can also be used to facilitate evaluation of computed results.

The orientation of beams in space can alternatively be specified using only nodes I and J if one also gives the **angle of rotation** θ of the cross section about the **element axis x**. (See Figure 5-14.) If $\theta = 0$, the element local **y-axis** is automatically calculated to be parallel to the global X-Y plane. In the previous example we get the same results if the third node is eliminated from the element definition since $\theta = 0$ corresponds to the desired orientation of the two elements in this case.

5-8 SUMMARY

ANSYS modeling of two and three-dimensional beam bending problems has been presented in this lesson and tutorials given to provide hands-on experience with this kind of analysis. The engineering theory of beam bending is the basis for the elements utilized here, and angular degrees of freedom (ROTX, etc.) are introduced for the first time since these variables are required for the calculation of the beam element neutral axis slope.

Transverse loads that cause bending also cause shearing deformations that may become important for short beams. The real property set for beams allows specification of the effective shear deformation area so that this behavior can be modeled when necessary.

Because they connect two node points, beam and truss elements are called 'line' elements in ANSYS. The Shell (plate) elements of the next lesson are the two-dimensional or surface equivalents of beams, connecting three or four nodes in a plane, they are loaded by forces transverse to their surface and experience bending in ways similar to beams.

5-9 PROBLEMS

Use 2-D beam models to find the maximum deflection (mm or inches) and bending stress (N/m^2 or psi) for the rectangular cross section single span beams of Problems 5-1 through 5-5 below. Use metric system units, **M,** or British system units, **B,** for problem formulation. Compare your computed results with those that you calculate from elementary beam theory (Use the uniform beam module in www.etbx.com, for example).

Length	$L = 3$ m	9.8 ft.
Elastic modulus	$E = 2.\text{E}11$ N/m^2	2.9E7 psi
Cross section Base	$b = 50$ mm	1.97 in
Cross section Height	$h = 150$ mm	5.9 in.
Distributed load	$w = 30$ kN/m	2055 lbf/ft
Point load	$P = 25$ kN	5620 lbf
Point moment	$M = 12$ kN-m	8852 ft-lbf

5-1 Simply supported beam (a) point load P at center, (b) uniformly distributed load w.

5-2 Fixed (cantilevered) at one end, free at the other, (a) point load P at free end, (b) uniformly distributed load w, (c) point moment M at free end, (d) linearly distributed load varying from w at the fixed end to zero at the free end.

5-3 Fixed (cantilevered) at both ends, (a) point load P at center, (b) uniformly distributed load w.

5-4 Fixed (cantilevered) at one end, simply supported at the other, (a) point load P at center, (b) uniformly distributed load w.

5-5 Find the maximum deflection and stress in the stepped steel cantilevered beam below with a point load on the free end. The segments are of equal length and the larger inertia is twice the smaller. Select your own material, geometric, and load values. Check the maximum bending stress with a simple hand calculation. The ANSYS calculated end deflection should be somewhere between that for a single beam of inertia I and that for one with an inertia 2I.

Figure P5-5

5-6 A stepped steel shaft with equal length segments of 16 inches, and 1.5 inch, 1 inch diameter cross sections is loaded with a 1000 lbf force in the middle and considered restrained from deflection and slope by the bearings at either end. (a) Compute the mid-span deflection and moment. (b) Compute the maximum bending stress at the step if the fillet radius is 0.25 inch. Do this by developing a 3D model of a segment of the shaft near

Figure P5-6

the step. Apply the moment found in (a) to the segment using equal and opposite forces. Assume that the 1000 lbf does not contribute significantly to the local stress distribution and can be ignored. Check your results against published stress concentration factors for this geometry.

5-7 Find the maximum stress and deflection of the 2-D frame shown if it has both columns fixed at ground level. The geometric, material, and distributed load parameters are the same as for the beam of Problem 5-1. There is a side load of w and also a uniformly distributed downward load w (not shown) on each horizontal beam.

Figure P5-7

5-8 Determine the maximum stress in the 'L'-beam of Figure 5-11 if a 10 lbf force is applied in the global Z direction in addition to the 5.0 lbf Y-direction force shown. Confirm the ANSYS result with a hand calculation.

5-9 Create a 3-dimensional model of a building frame using two frames like that of Problem 5-7, the second displaced 3 m in the Z-direction from the first. The second frame is loaded like the first and connected to it by with beams at the 4 and 8 m levels. The connecting beams (same properties as the others) have distributed loads $2w$ N/m. Find maximum stress and displacement.

5-10 The tower in the figure has a right triangle base and is loaded by two 5000 lbf forces parallel to the direction of the 8 ft side of the triangle. Find the maximum displacement and stress if the tower is made from steel pipe with a 4.5 inch OD and a wall thickness of 0.337 inches. The three legs are firmly anchored at ground level, so the three base triangle lines do not need to be elements of the model. Use BEAM4 or PIPE16 (needs only two nodes to define) elements.

Figure P5-10

Lesson 6

Shells

6-1 OVERVIEW

Shell (or plate) elements can resist loads in all directions and become extremely versatile modeling tools for thin planar and curved surfaces. The exercises below demonstrate

◆ Modeling flat plates with ANSYS shell elements.

◆ Evaluating shell element solution accuracy.

◆ Solving problems involving thin walled structures.

6-2 INTRODUCTION

Shell elements behave as the two-dimensional equivalents of beams. They connect three or four node points in a plane and when loaded by forces transverse to their surfaces, experience bending about the X-axis and about the Y-axis. These deformations cause bending stresses that vary linearly through the shell thickness. Transverse loads can also cause twisting as well as bending. The **middle surface** of the plate is a plane of zero bending strain as is the neutral axis plane of a beam.

Figure 6-1 Shell

We will use the terms plate and shell interchangeably in this discussion. As with beams, if the plate thickness is a tenth or less than the length dimension, pure bending dominates, but for greater thickness to length ratios, through-the-thickness shearing deformation begins to become important as well as bending.

Four and eight-node quad shell elements are provided in the ANSYS element library. They support bending, shearing and in-plane loadings. Like beams, the in-plane or membrane loadings are not coupled with the bending loadings for linear analysis.

Plate element theory does not naturally supply stiffness to resist a torque applied normal to the shell surface, but this deficiency is overcome by introducing a physically reasonable stiffness parameter in the mathematical formulation in order to provide elements that resist loading in all six degrees of freedom at a each node.

Figure 6-2 Shell degrees of freedom

6-3 SQUARE PLATE

As an example of the use of ANSYS shell elements, consider a **10 inch** by **10 inch** 304 steel plate that **is 0.1 inch thick** and has a **1.0 lbf force** applied at its center. The plate is **simply supported** on all sides

Figure 6-3 Simply supported, point-loaded plate.

6-4 TUTORIAL 6A - SQUARE PLATE

Objective. Determine the deflection at the load point as a function of the number of elements used per side to model the plate and find the von Mises stress distribution.

The plate has two planes of symmetry, so we model just one quadrant and apply appropriate boundary conditions. For starters, use the ANSYS simple **four-node** element, **SHELL63** for the model.

Start ANSYS and select the working directory for this problem then select the element.

1. Main Menu > Preprocessor > Element Type > Add/Edit/Delete > Add > Structural Shell > Elastic 4 Node 63 > Close

Specify the plate thickness

2. Main Menu > Preprocessor > Real Constants > Add/Edit/Delete > Add > Shell Thickness at Node I Enter **0.1 > OK > Close**

3. Enter material properties for 304 steel, E = 2.8E7, prxy = 0.29

Create a 5 inch x 5 inch area (one quarter of the 10 x 10 plate).

4. Main Menu > Preprocessor > Modeling > Create > Areas > Rectangle > By 2 Corners > Enter 0.0, 0.0, 5.0, 5.0 > OK

First set the size controls so that 2 divisions per line are created. Then mesh the area to create 2 elements per edge.

5. Main Menu > Preprocessor > Meshing > Size Controls > Manual Size > Lines > All Lines > NDIV Number of element divisions > Enter 2 (Also set KYNDIV SIZE; NDIV can be changed to No.) > OK

6. Main Menu > Preprocessor > Meshing > Mesh > Areas > Free (Select the 5 x 5 square)

Figure 6-4 Quadrant of simply supported plate.

Now apply boundary conditions and loads. The global axis system is located at the center of the plate. Edges 1 and 2 (at $x = 5.0$ and $y = 5.0$) are **Simply Supported**. This means that there is no displacement in the vertical direction and that the slope normal to the edge is zero. Edges 3 and 4 are along lines of symmetry, and the plate must have a symmetric deformation shape across the lines of symmetry.

Edge 1

7. Main Menu > Preprocessor > Loads > Define Loads > Apply > Structural > Displacement > On Lines > Select Edge 1 > Set UZ = 0 > OK Then repeat and set ROTX = 0.

Edge 2

8. Main Menu > Preprocessor > Loads > Define Loads > Apply > Structural > Displacement > On Lines > Select Edge 2 > Set UZ = 0 > OK Then repeat and set ROTY = 0.

Edge 3

9. Main Menu > Preprocessor > Loads > Define Loads > Apply > Structural > Displacement > On Lines > Select Edge 3 > Set UX = 0 > OK Then repeat and set ROTY = 0.

Edge 4

10. Main Menu > Preprocessor > Loads > Define Loads > Apply > Structural > Displacement > On Lines > Select Edge 4 > Set UY = 0 > OK Then repeat and set ROTX = 0.

Apply one-quarter of the total load to the **keypoint** at the origin of coordinates.

11. Main Menu > Preprocessor > Loads > Define Loads > Apply > Structural > Force/Moment > On Keypoints > Select Keypoint at origin. For FZ enter -0.25 > OK

Perform the solution

12. Main Menu > Solution > Solve > Current LS > OK

Post processing

13. Main Menu > General Postproc > Plot Results > Deformed Shape > Def + undeformed

Figure 6-5 Deflected shape.

Plot the contours of vertical displacement over the plate.

14. Main Menu > General Postproc > Plot Results > Contour Plot > Nodal Solu > DOF Solution > Z-Component of displacement > OK

Figure 6-6 UZ contours.

List values or use the results viewer to determine the deflection at the center of the plate.

15. Main Menu > General Postproc > List Results > Nodal Solu > DOF Solution > Z-Component of displacement > OK

The maximum deflection (at the center of the plate - node 1 for this model) is **-0.47283E-03 inches.** The **theoretical solution** to this problem gives a deflection value of **0.452E-3 inches**. Thus, our mesh is not fine enough with this element to give an accurate deflection solution. As verification, plot the calculated **von Mises Stress.** SEQV is the combination of SX, SY, and SXY bending and shearing stresses at the surface of the plate.

16. Main Menu > General Postproc > Plot Results > Contour Plot > Element Solu > Stress > von Mises stress > OK

Figure 6-7 von Mises stress contours.

The discontinuities in stress contours indicate an inaccurate stress solution for this mesh and element. To improve the accuracy, clear the mesh (**Preprocessor > Meshing > Clear > Areas**) and remesh with 4 elements per edge. Then repeat with 8 elements per edge, etc. The deflection results are shown below.

Elements per edge	Deflection
2	0.473E-3
4	0.461E-3
8	0.457E-3
Theory	0.452E-3

We observe that the 8-elements-per-edge mesh produces deflection with an **error of only 1.1 percent** when compared to thin plate theory. Also notice that the maximum displacement is converging from above, meaning that the shell elements are **softer** than the theoretical solution we are using for comparison.

Contours of vertical deflection UZ and von Mises stress for the 8 by 8 mesh are shown below. The stress contours are now much smoother in comparison with the first mesh. However, the element solution stress plots show discontinuities near the point-load singularity at the center of the plate as we would expect.

Figure 6-8 UZ and von Mises stress contours for 8 x 8 mesh.

Since the stresses are proportional to the spatial derivatives (x and y) of the displacements, the stresses generally have greater error than the displacements.

It is easier to visualize the slope boundary conditions for the full plate, and with a problem this simple, you might want to use the complete plate. If so, you would compute contours such as those shown below and could use symmetry (or lack of it) to help evaluate the validity of your model.

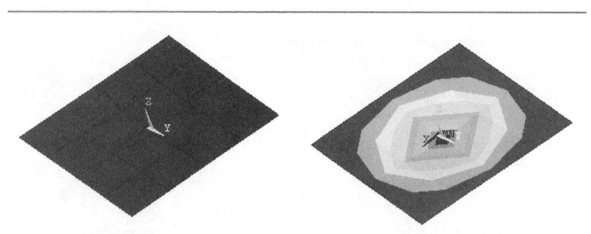

Figure 6-9 Displaced shape and UZ contours for full plate model.

To obtain yet greater accuracy for this problem, increase the mesh density or switch to the more accurate eight-node **SHELL93** element, or do both.

The ANSYS shell elements are capable of modeling a wide range of practical problems as shown in the next example.

6-5 TUTORIAL 6B - CHANNEL BEAM

Objective: Find the deformations and stresses in a cantilevered thin walled channel subject to an end load. The 6 x 2 x 0.2 inch thick steel channel shown below is 30 inches long and has a total load of 1.0 lbf equally divided among the four corner points on the right end as shown.

Figure 6-10 Channel model

The following text file is used to create the geometry.

```
/FILNAM,Tutorial6B
/title, Channel geometry

/prep7
! Create geometry
k, 1,  0.,  -3., 0.          ! Keypoint 1 is at -3.0, 0.0
k, 2,  0.,   3., 0.
k, 3,  0.,  -3., 2.
k, 4,  0.,   3., 2.
k, 5, 30.,  -3., 0.
k, 6, 30.,   3., 0.
k, 7, 30.,  -3., 2.
k, 8, 30.,   3., 2.

L, 1, 2     ! Line connecting keypoints 1 & 2
L, 2, 4
L, 3, 1
L, 4, 8
L, 2, 6
L, 6, 8
L, 6, 5
L, 7, 5
L, 1, 5
L, 3, 7

AL, 1, 5, 7, 9  ! Area defined by lines 1, 5, 7, 9
AL, 2, 5, 6, 4
AL, 3, 9, 8, 10
```

Start ANSYS, select the working directory for this problem and select a job name.

1. Read the text file to create the geometry **File > Read Input from ...**

We will use the eight-node **SHELL93** element for this example.

2. Main Menu > Preprocessor > Element Type > Add/Edit/Delete > Add > Structural Shell > Elastic 8 Node 93 > Close

Specify the plate thickness.

3. Main Menu > Preprocessor > Real Constants > Add/Edit/Delete > Add > Shell Thickness at Node I Enter **0.2 > OK > Close**

4. Enter **E = 3.E7** and **prxy = 0.3** material properties for steel.

Use size controls and mapped meshing to create **2** elements along each flange, **4** elements through the web, and **10** elements along the length.

For the flanges

5. Main Menu > Preprocessor > Meshing > Size Controls > Manual Size > Lines > Picked Lines > (Select the short edges of upper and lower flanges) **NDIV Number of element divisions > Enter 2 > OK**

Repeat for the web height and length edges then mesh all three areas.

6. Main Menu > Preprocessor > Meshing > Mesh > Areas > Mapped > 3 or 4 sided > Pick All

Figure 6-11 Channel quad mesh.

7. Restrain all DOF along the lines on the left end and apply **Fy = -0.25 lbf** to the four keypoints on the right end.

8. Solve and open the **Postprocessor** to plot the deformed shape and the von Mises stresses as shown below.

Figure 6-12 Displaced shape and von Mises stress contours.

The observed twisting occurs because the resultant end load is not applied through the shear center of the thin-walled cross section. The point loads cause the high stresses on the right end, and if you zoom in you see that the mesh also needs refinement at points away from the ends to obtain better accuracy.

6-6 SUMMARY

Thin plate or shell elements find applications in many practical situations as illustrated by the tutorials in this lesson. They are particularly useful for the analysis of parts such as structural angle brackets, automotive hoods or trunk lid attachments and similar thin components with fairly complex shape. In these cases shells may offer a modeling and analysis advantage over comparable models that use solid elements.

6-7 PROBLEMS

6-1 Duplicate the analysis of Tutorial 6A but change the boundary conditions to **fixed** on **all edges** and the loading to a **uniform pressure** of 1.0 psi. Compare your results to results calculated from published solutions for thin plate deformation and stress.

6-2 Repeat Tutorial 6B but use a T, H, L, or I thin-walled section. Load symmetric sections off center so as to cause twisting.

6-3 Use a solid modeler to develop the geometry of an angle bracket or hood hinge attachment. Import the middle surface of the solid model into ANSYS, then formulate suitable loading and boundary conditions for analysis with ANSYS shell elements.

6-4 Solve any of the tutorials or problems from this lesson with solid tetrahedron or brick elements and compare the results of the two kinds of modeling.

6-5 A vertical thin-walled conical tube is completely fixed at its base and is loaded by a uniformly distributed horizontal force at its top. Use SHELL93 elements for modeling and determine the transverse deflection at the top and the maximum von Mises stress at mid height if it is made of steel. Select your own dimensions, material properties, and loads.

Figure P6-5

Lesson 7

Heat
Transfer
&
Thermal Stress

7-1 OVERVIEW

Heretofore we have considered only problems in structural and continuum mechanics. ANSYS capabilities also include modeling of problems involving the behavior of thermal, fluid, electric and magnetic systems. Lesson 7 demonstrates

♦ Determining temperature distributions in conduction/convection problems.

♦ Using temperature distributions to find thermal stresses.

7-2 INTRODUCTON

Linear thermal conduction/convection problems are formulated using the finite element approach with temperature as the single degree-of-freedom variable at each node in the mesh and with the material conduction properties used to form the thermal 'stiffness matrix' to be solved.

The ANSYS library includes one-, two-, and three-dimensional thermal elements for modeling problems of interest to practicing engineers. The temperature distributions found at each thermal analysis node can be stored for use with the equivalent structural model for use as nodal 'inputs' for finding stresses caused by temperature changes.

7-3 HEAT TRANSFER

Triangular and quadrilateral thermal elements are provided to perform thermal analysis for planar and axisymmetric models, while tetrahedron and brick shaped elements are available for three-dimensional problems. A correspondence in the number of nodes and their locations between thermal and structural models allows switching between the two types of analysis without creating a new mesh.

We start by solving a conduction/convection problem defined in two-dimensions. The theoretical solution for this problem is available for comparison.

7-4 TUTORIAL 7A – TEMPERATURE DISTRIBUTION IN A CYLINDER

Objective: We wish to compute the temperature distribution in a long steel cylinder with inner radius 5 inches and outer radius 10 inches. The interior of the cylinder is kept at 75 deg F, and heat is lost on the exterior by convection to a fluid whose temperature is 40 deg F. The **convection coefficient is 2.E-4 BTU/sec-sq.in-F** and the **thermal conductivity** for steel is taken to be **8.09 E-4 BTU/sec-in-F**.

Figure 7-1 Cylinder with internal temperature and exterior convection.

1. Start ANSYS and assign a job name to the project. **Run Interactive > set working directory and jobname.**

2. Main Menu > Preferences > Select **Thermal** and **h-method > OK** (This is a thermal problem.)

Select the eight-node thermal quad element. (Scroll down the list of elements to find thermal.)

3. Main Menu > Preprocessor > Element Type > Add/Edit/Delete > Add > Thermal Solid > 8 node 77 > OK > Close

4. Main Menu > Preprocessor > Material Props > Material Models > Thermal > Conductivity > Isotropic > Enter **KXX = 8.09 E-4** (BTU/sec-in-F) **> OK > Close window.**

Create the geometry

5. Recognizing the symmetry of the problem, a quadrant of a section through the cylinder is created using ANSYS area creation tools. **Main Menu > Preprocessor > Modeling > Create > Areas > Circle > Partial Annulus**

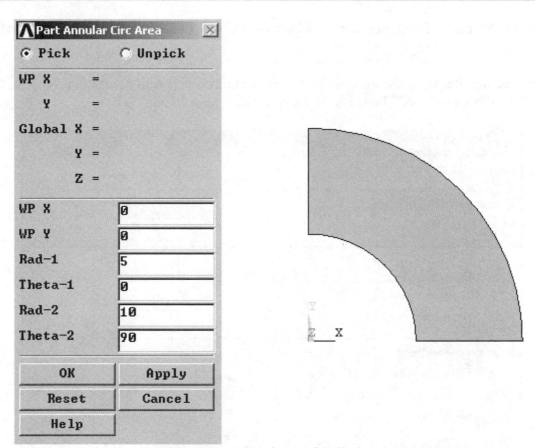

Figure 7-2 Quadrant of cylinder.

6. Set the number of line divisions to 5 radially and 8 circumferentially and use mapped meshing, 3 or 4 sided areas, to create the 5 by 8 mesh shown.

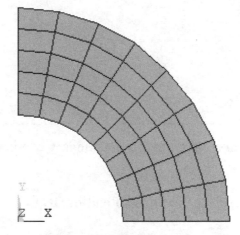

Figure 7-3 Quad mesh.

7. Main Menu > Preprocessor > Loads > Define Loads > Apply > Thermal > Temperatures > On Lines Select the interior boundary and set the temperature to **75**.

8. Main Menu > Preprocessor > Loads > Define Loads > Apply > Thermal > Convection > On Lines

Select the line defining the outer surface; set the convection film coefficient to 2e-4 and the bulk fluid temp to 40. (Leave VALJ and VAL2J fields blank.) **OK**

Figure 7-4 Convection boundary condition.

To account for symmetry, select the **vertical** and **horizontal lines of symmetry** and set the heat flux to zero.

9. Main Menu > Preprocessor > Loads > Define Loads > Apply > Thermal > Heat Flux > On Lines > 0 > OK

Apply HFLUX on lines

[SFL] Apply HFLUX on lines as a   Constant value ▼

If Constant value then:

VALI   Heat flux   0

    Optional HFLUX values at end J of line

    (leave blank for uniform HFLUX)

VALJ   Heat flux

OK   Cancel   Help

Figure 7-5 Zero flux on lines of symmetry.

Use **PlotCtrls > [/PSF] Surface Load Symbols > Convect FilmCoef > Show pres as > Arrows** to view the convection boundary conditions. Or **List > Loads > Surface > On All Lines** to view all surface boundary conditions.

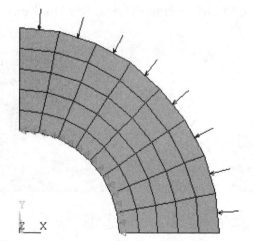

Figure 7-6 Temperature and convection boundary conditions.

10. Main Menu > Solution > Solve > Current LS

11. Main Menu > General Postprocessor > Plot Results > Contour Plot > Nodal Solu > DOF Solution > Nodal Temperature > OK

Figure 7-7 Temperature distribution.

The maximum temperature is on the interior and is the specified 75 F. On the outside wall the minimum temperature is found to be about **53 F**. These results can be verified using closed form solutions from heat transfer theory.

12. Save your work.

Because of its symmetry, this problem could have been solved with a much smaller model, say a 15 degree wedge by setting the heat flux on the cut faces to zero.

Figure 7-8 Temperature distribution for wedge model.

7-5 THERMAL STRESS

Objective: To determine the stress in an object due to a temperature change.

When a temperature change occurs in an object, its coefficient of thermal expansion causes an expansion or contraction of the object depending upon whether the temperature increases or decreases. If the object is unrestrained, there is no stress associated with this free motion. On the other hand, if the object is subject to restraint against the thermally induced movement, a stress will occur.

The finite element method provides tools for the solution of thermal stress problems. The temperature changes can be uniform throughout the body or distributed due to thermal conditions such as those in the previous tutorial.

7-6 TUTORIAL 7B – UNIFORM TEMPERATURE CHANGE

Consider a block of material (1) surrounded by a second material (2) as shown in the figure below. The composite is subjected to a temperature change so that both regions attain a uniform final temperature throughout. Find the stresses that result if the initial state is stress free. We're missing a couple of components here, but this is similar to the situation that occurs during the encapsulation of computer chips.

Figure 7-9 Encapsulation model.

Assume a representative geometry of about 6 x 25 mm for a plane stress model. The text file below generates the **upper right quadrant** of the geometry and includes hypothetical material properties with different elastic moduli and different CTE's, coefficients of thermal expansion, *alpx* for the two components.

```
/FILNAM,Tutorial7B
/title, Chip geometry

/prep7
! Create geometry
k, 1,    0,   0.        ! Keypoint 1 is at 0.0, 0.0
k, 2,  9.5,   0.
k, 3, 12.5,   0.
k, 4,    0,  1.6
k, 5,  9.5,  1.6
k, 6, 12.5,  1.6
k, 7,    0,  3.2
k, 8,  9.5,  3.2
k, 9, 12.5,  3.2
```

```
L, 1, 2     ! Line connecting keypoints 1 & 2
L, 2, 3
L, 4, 5
L, 5, 6
L, 7, 8
L, 8, 9
L, 1, 4
L, 2, 5
L, 3, 6
L, 4, 7
L, 5, 8
L, 6, 9

AL, 1, 8, 3, 7    ! Area defined by lines 1, 8, 3, 7
AL, 2, 9, 4, 8
AL, 3, 11, 5, 10
AL, 4, 12, 6, 11

mp, ex, 1, 3.e4        ! Material 1 properties, including CTE
mp, prxy, 1, 0.3
mp, alpx, 1, 10.3e-6

mp, ex, 2, 2.5e3
mp, prxy, 2, 0.3
mp, alpx, 2, 100.e-6
```

1. Start ANSYS, etc. **Set preferences to Structural**. (This is a **structural problem** with a **thermal loading**.) Read in the text file defining the upper right quadrant of the geometry shown in the previous figure. Turn on **area numbering** and **plot the areas**.

Figure 7-10 Areas.

2. Select the **8-node quad 183** structural element (plane stress default).

3. Main Menu > Preprocessor > Meshing > Mesh Attributes > Picked Areas > Select area A1 > OK > Area Attributes (select area A1 to be Material 1) **> OK**

4. Repeat specifying areas **A2, A3, A4** to be Material 2.

5. Use **manual size controls** to divide the interior horizontal and vertical line segments into **12, 4, 4,** and **4 divisions**. Then **Mapped Mesh > 3 or 4 sided > Pick All**

Check to see that the material assignments are correct.

6. Utility Menu > PlotCntls > Numbering > Elem / Attribute numbering > Material Numbers > OK

Figure 7-11 Two-material mesh.

7. Apply **symmetric displacement boundary conditions** along bottom edge (UY = 0) and left edge (UX = 0).

Apply a **uniform temperature change** of **-150 deg C** representing a cool down during the encapsulation operation from the initial stress-free state.

8. Main Menu > Preprocessor > Loads > Define Loads > Apply > Structural > Temperature > On Areas > Pick All > Enter -150 > OK

9. Save your work, Solve, and go to postprocessor.

10. Plot Results The **deformed shape** (note shrinkage) and the **first principal stress, S1,** are shown in the two figures below.

Figure 7-12 Deformed shape.

Figure 7-13 First principal stress.

The stress plot shows the singularity at the interior right angle of the composite object. The largest principal stress in magnitude is **S3**.

7-7 TUTORIAL 7C – THERMAL STRESS

Objective: In this exercise we wish to first compute the temperature distribution in the vessel below, and then compute the thermal stresses that result after the thermal changes assuming an initial stress-free state.

A steel cylinder with inner radius 5 inches and outer radius 10 inches is 40 inches long and has spherical end caps. The interior of the cylinder is kept at 75 deg F, and heat is lost on the exterior by convection to a fluid whose temperature is 40 deg F. The convection film coefficient is 2E-4 BTU/sec-sq.in-F. Calculate the stresses in the cylinder caused by the new temperature distribution.

The problem is solved in two steps. First, the geometry is created, the heat transfer problem is modeled and solved, and the results of the heat transfer analysis (temperatures) are saved in a file, '**jobname.RTH**' (**R**esults **TH**ermal analysis).

Next the heat transfer boundary conditions and loads are removed from the mesh, the element type is changed from 'thermal' to 'structural', and the nodal temperatures which were saved in the file 'jobname.RTH' are recalled and applied as thermal loads.

1. Start ANSYS. Run Interactive > set working directory and jobname. (Set the jobname to Tutorial7C. This step is **important** since you will need to locate Tutorial7C.RTH after the thermal analysis has been performed.)

2. Main Menu > Preferences > Select **Structural &Thermal & h-method > OK**

Enter the structural and thermal material properties, **E**, **prxy**, **alpx**, and **KXX**.

3. Main Menu > Preprocessor > Material Props > Material Models > Material Number 1 > Structural > Linear > Elastic > Isotropic > EX = 3.E7, PRXY = 0.3 > OK

Thermal Expansion > Secant Coefficient > Isotropic > ALPX = 6.5E-6 > OK

Thermal > Conductivity > Isotropic > KXX = 8.09 e-4 > OK > Close

4. Generate a quadrant of a section through the cylinder using ANSYS area creation tools. We will use **axisymmetric** modeling techniques.

At point $x = 5.0$, $y = 0.0$, create a **5 by 10 inch rectangle**. At center $x = 0.0$, $y = 10.0$, create a **partial annulus** R1 = 5, Theta1 = 0, R2 =10, Theta2 = 90. **Glue** the two areas together to form two four-edged regions suitable for mapped meshing. (**Modeling > Operate > Booleans > Glue > Areas**). Next select the thermal quad element.

Figure 7-14 Quadrant of vessel.

5. Main Menu > Preprocessor > Element Type > Add/Edit/Delete > Add > Thermal > Solid 8 node 77 > OK   (Scroll down to locate it.)

Options > Element behavior K3 Axisymmetric > OK > Close

6. Use mapped meshing to create the **5** by **20** mesh shown below.

7. Main Menu > Preprocessor > Loads > Define Loads > Apply > Thermal > Temperature > On Lines

Select the line on the interior and set the temperature to 75.

8. Main Menu > Preprocessor > Loads > Define Loads > Apply > Thermal > Convection > On Lines

Select the line defining the outer surface and set the
constant **Film coefficient = 2e-4** and the fluid **Bulk
temperature = 40**.

**9. Main Menu > Preprocessor > Loads > Define
Loads > Apply > Thermal > Heat Flux > On
Lines**

Select the bottom horizontal line of symmetry and
set the **heat flux** to zero.

Use **PlotCtrls > Surface Load Symbols > Heat
Fluxes** & **Show pres as > Contours** to view the
flux boundary conditions. Or **List > Loads >
Surface > On All Lines**.

Figure 7-15 Boundary conditions.

10. Main Menu > Solution > Solve > Current LS > OK   (Ignore the warning
'convection on or near a zero radius face'. Plot the temperature distribution.)

**11. Main Menu > General Postprocessor > Plot Results > Contour Plot > Nodal Solu
> DOF Solution > Temperature > OK**

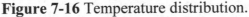

Figure 7-16 Temperature distribution.

The temperature on the interior is 75 deg F as it should be and on the outside wall it is found to be about 50 F. **Save the temperature results for use later.**

12. Utility Menu > File > Save Jobname.db   (Check in your working directory.)

Delete all of the thermal loads (boundary conditions).

13. Main Menu > Preprocessor > Loads > Define Loads > Delete > All Load Data > All Loads & Opts. > OK

Switch the element type from thermal to structural.

14. Main Menu > Preprocessor > Element Type > Switch Elem Type   (Select **Thermal to Struc**) **> OK** (This changes the element to the compatible 8 node structural element.)

Figure 7-17 Switch element type to structural.

Figure 7-18 Warning of element change.

Close the warning message window but be sure to set the PLANE183 structural element options to **axisymmetric**.

15. Main Menu > Preprocessor > Element Type > Add/Edit/Delete > PLANE183 > Options > Element behavior K3 Axisymmetric > OK > Close.   Plot > Elements

Now apply the structural boundary conditions and loads. (If the vessel had an internal and/or external pressure, it would be added here. For now we focus on the thermal effects only.)

16. Main Menu > Preprocessor > Loads > Define Loads > Apply > Structural > Displacement > On Lines

(Set UY = 0 on the bottom horizontal line of symmetry. You can use the Utility menu **List > Loads > DOF Constraints** or **PlotCtrls > Symbols > All Applied BCs** to check the model.)

Now read in the nodal temperatures computed during the thermal analysis step.

17. Main Menu > Preprocessor > Loads > Define Loads > Apply > Temperature > From Thermal Analy. Browse and select **Tutorial7C.RTH.** (If you don't find it, check the current jobname by trying to change the jobname. Also use Utility Menu > List > Loads > Body > On All Nodes to check the thermal loads.)

Solve the structural problem.

18. Main Menu > Solution > Solve > Current LS

19. Main Menu > General Postproc > Plot Results > Contour Plot > Element Solu > Stress > von Mises stress > OK

```
ELEMENT SOLUTION
STEP=1
SUB =1
TIME=1
SEQV      (NOAVG)
DMX =.007662
SMN =343.941
SMX =4519
```

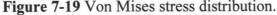

```
343.941           1272            2200           3127           4055
        807.854           1736           2664           3591           4519
```

Figure 7-19 Von Mises stress distribution.

The von Mises stress is seen to be a maximum of about 4500 psi in the end cap on the interior of the cylinder and would govern a yield-based design decision for a ductile steel.

Note that a finer mesh is generally required to get adequate accuracy for the stress analysis problem than is required for the thermal problem, so one must plan ahead in mesh design for the first phase of an analysis of the type discussed in this tutorial.

7-8 SUMMARY

The tutorials in this lesson illustrate the solution of thermal conduction/convection problems as well as the determination of thermal stresses arising from uniform or non-uniform temperature distributions. Although only planar and axisymmetric examples were considered, the extension to three-dimensional analysis follows directly from the examples here and those of Lesson 4.

7-9 PROBLEMS

7-1 Find the temperature distribution in the plate of Tutorial 2A if the hole is maintained at a temperature of 100 deg. C and the edges are exposed to a fluid at 0 deg C with a convection film coefficient of 20 W/m^2-C. The material conductivity is 18 W/m-C. Assume no variation on the Z-direction so that a two-dimensional model is sufficient.

7-2 The shaft described in Problem 5-6 is subjected to a uniform 150 deg. F temperature rise. Use an axisymmetric model to find the maximum axial stress due to thermal effects only.

7-3 The pressure vessel of Lesson 3 is subjected to the thermal conditions of Tutorial 7C. Find the maximum von Mises stress due to thermal loading. Repeat with thermal and pressure loading.

7-4 Repeat 7-3 using the vessel of Problem 3-1.

7-5 Repeat Problem 7-1 but now assume the front and back surfaces of the plate are subject to convection the way fins on a cylindrical tube are used to cool (or heat) a fluid within the tube. Use three-dimensional modeling to determine the temperature distribution in the plate.

7-6 A composite wall is composed of two layers as shown. The conductivities are 0.05 W/cm-C for the 8 cm layer and 0.4 W/cm-C for the 3 cm layer. The free surface of the thick layer is maintained at 20 C. Convection at the free surface of the thin layer occurs with a film coefficient of 0.1 W/cm^2-C and free stream temperature of –5 C.

Find the temperature at the interface of the two layers. Use a two-dimensional model of rectangular elements of arbitrary *y*-direction height (say 1 cm) with zero heat flux in the *y* direction on the top and bottom boundaries.

Figure P7-6

7-7 An 8 in diameter steel disk 0.1 inches in thickness has a 2 in diameter hole located 1 inch radially from its center. The hole is maintained at 75 F and the exterior loses heat by convection to an environment whose temperature is 40 F. The convection film coefficient is 2.0E-4 BTU/sec-in^2-F.

Find the temperature distribution and the value and location of the maximum von Mises stress, the maximum principal stress, and the maximum principal strain if the disk is initially in a stress-free state before the thermal conditions are applied.

Figure P7-7

7-8 Solve problem 7-2 using a three-dimensional model.

NOTES:

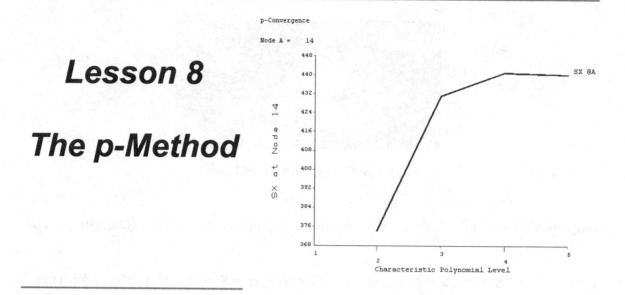

Lesson 8

The p-Method

8-1 OVERVIEW

This lesson uses a plane stress problem to give a brief introduction to the p-method.

8-2 INTRODUCTION

In Lesson 2 we discussed the relationship between the element displacement approximation polynomial and the ability of the element to represent sharp stress gradients. In all previous lessons the elements used were based upon second order polynomial functions at most, and we used the **h-method** (more elements of smaller size) to obtain the desired accuracy. Here 'h' refers to a characteristic length of elements that is decreased as we pack more and more elements into regions of high stress gradient.

Another approach to accuracy improvement is to increase the polynomial order of the elements being used and to change the order selectively, that is, only the elements in the mesh that need it have their polynomial order increased. This is called the **p-method**, where 'p' refers to the polynomial order. ANSYS provides the user with p-elements and methods to automatically control the solution process so as to arrive at an answer with predetermined convergence characteristics.

8-3 TUTORIAL 8A – PLATE WITH HOLE, P-METHOD SOLUTION

A **20 x 40 x 1 inch thick steel plate** with a **10 inch diameter** central hole and subjected to a **tensile axial pressure loading of 100 psi** along its short edge is used to illustrate this approach. Use E = 3.e7 psi and prxy = 0.3.

Figure 8-1 Plate with central hole.

Objective: Accurately determine the maximum axial (SX) stress in the plate using the p-method.

1. Start ANSYS and select **Main Menu > Preferences > Structural, p-Method Struct.**

2. Main Menu > Preprocessor > Element Type > Add/Edit/Delete > Add > select 2D Triangle 146 > OK > Close

This selects a p-method, plane-stress element with a default unit thickness.

3. Create the geometry of a quadrant of the plate and give it a mesh as discussed in previous examples. Add loads and boundary conditions to arrive at the following model.

Figure 8-2 Mesh, boundary conditions and load.

With the p-method selected under preferences, the program will **solve the FEM problem repeatedly,** automatically adjusting the polynomial level in the elements until a specified solution quantity ceases to change to within some specified tolerance.

The **default convergence quantity** is the **total global strain energy.** The **default criteria** is that the model strain energy stabilize to the point that its value for a new polynomial level is within 5 percent of the value found using the previous polynomial level. To solve the problem using the default convergence criteria, select as before:

4. Main Menu > Solution > Solve > Current LS

Read and plot the results.

5. Main Menu > General Post Processor > Read Results > Last Set

6. Main Menu > General Post Processor > Plot Results > Contour Plot > Element Solution > X-Component of stress > OK

The problem is solved for each p-level considered, so we want to plot the last solution.

Figure 8-3 SX stress contours.

SXmax is found to be about **438 psi**. The initial p-level is automatically set to 2 for each element. To see what the final p-levels are, select **Plot Results > p-Method > p-Levels**.

Figure 8-4 P-levels.

The p-level was advanced from 2 to 3 for all elements except one. To evaluate the convergence, select **Plot Results > p-Method > p-Convergence > All specified > OK.**

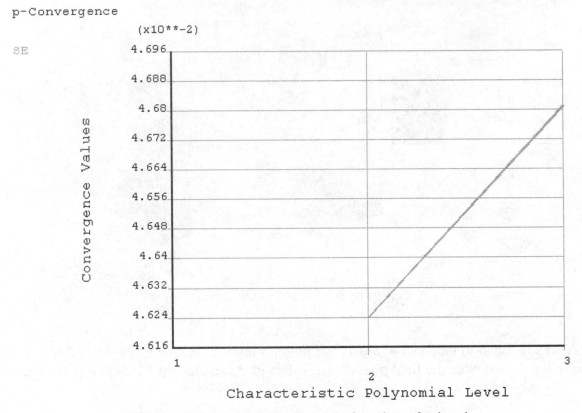

Figure 8-5 Total strain energy as a function of p-level.

Using the default convergence criteria gives a slight discontinuity in some of the stress contours across element boundaries, but the total strain energy looks as though it would continue to change if the p-levels were increased further. To increase the accuracy, we will employ a different convergence criteria and solve the problem again.

The quantity of interest in this problem is the maximum stress in the vicinity of the hole; therefore we repeat the solution using **SX at the point of highest stress** as the

convergence criterion. We will replace the global convergence quantity (strain energy) with a local quantity (SX). (First **Plot > Elements** so we can see the mesh again.)

7. Main Menu > Preprocessor > Loads > Load Step Opts > p-Method > Convergence Criteria > Replace > Local for solids > OK

Figure 8-6 Replace default convergence criteria.

Figure 8-7 Add/Replace convergence criteria.

Pick the node where the maximum stress will occur > **OK**.

Figure 8-8 Select the point of maximum SX.

8. Change the convergence tolerance, TOLER, from 5% to 1% and select Stress X-direction SX > OK > Close

Figure 8-9 Add p-convergence criteria.

9. Solve the problem again. **Main Menu > Solution > Solve > Current LS**

Read and plot the last solution set of results.

10. Main Menu > General Post Processor > Read Results > Last Set; > Plot Results > Contour Plot > Element Solution > X-Component of stress > OK

87.823   188.714   289.606   390.498
        138.269   239.16   340.052   440.944

Figure 8-10 SX stress contours.

Note the smoothness of these stress contours near the hole. The value of SXmax is now about 441 psi, an increase of less than 1 percent over the value found using global strain energy as the convergence criterion. The p-level distribution in the mesh is shown next.

Figure 8-11 P-level variation within the mesh.

To obtain the requested convergence, it was necessary to use p-levels of 5 in many of the elements. The convergence history of SX at the specified node is shown next.

11. Plot Results > p-Method > p-Convergence > Stress X-direction SX > OK

p-Convergence

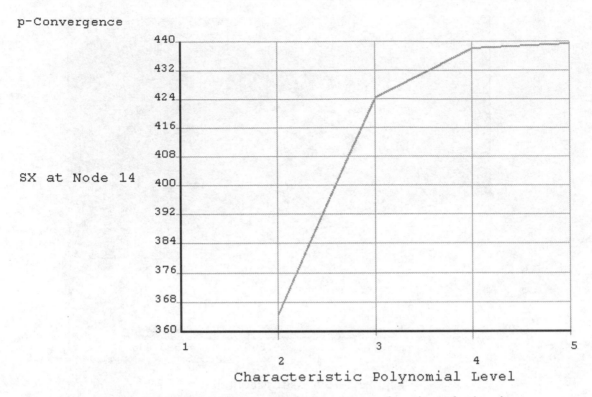

Figure 8-12 Stress SX at specified node as a function of p-level.

The SX stress component at the hole is seen to converge nicely with p-level variation. The **maximum p-level** available for the elements in ANSYS is **8**. If using p-levels of 8 does not provide the desired convergence, a more refined initial mesh should be created and the problem solved again.

8-4 SUMMARY

This lesson illustrates the use of the p-method to control the accuracy of ANSYS FEM stress calculations. While the change with p refinement is not dramatic in the example used here, the extension to more demanding problems seems evident. Multiple criteria can be used to control the solution sequence, and the p-level will be changed until either all criteria are met or the p-level capacity of the current mesh is exhausted. In addition we note that the techniques discussed here are equally applicable to axisymmetric and three-dimensional problems.

8-5 PROBLEMS

Use the p-method to solve the following:

8-1 The problem in Tutorial 2B

8-2 Problem 2-2

8-3 Problem 2-3

8-2 Problem 2-5

8-4 Problem 2-6

8-5 Problem 2-7

8-6 Problem 2-8

Problems 8-8 through 8-11 can be solved either as axisymmetric or as three-dimensional problems.

8-7 The problem of Tutorial 3A.

8-8 Problem 3-3

8-9 Problem 3-4

8-10 Problem 3-5

8-11 Problem 3-7

NOTES:

Lesson 9

Selected Topics

9-1 OVERVIEW

Selected topics not included in previous Lessons are included here for your reference.

9-2 LOADING DUE TO GRAVITY

The loading due to the weight of the structure in many of the examples we have analyzed so far was small in comparison to the applied loads and therefore was neglected in the analysis. If we want to consider the loading due to gravity, we need to make two additions to the input data: (1) Be sure to specify the **mass density** when entering material data and (2) Indicate the magnitude of the **acceleration of gravity** and its direction with respect to the global axis system for the problem.

To consider loading due to weight in Tutorial 1A for example, we would make the following additions to the text file. The length units for this analysis are inches, so we stick to inches. The **weight density** for steel is about 0.283 lbf/in^3. To find mass density, divide the weight density by the acceleration of gravity at the location on earth where the weighing took place, usually taken to be 386 in/sec^2 at sea level. Thus the **mass density** for steel in the British system inch units is

$$\rho = 0.283/386 = 0.0007331 \text{ lbf-sec}^2/\text{in}^4 = 0.7331\text{E-3 lbf-sec}^2/\text{in}^4. \quad \text{(about 7833 kg/m}^3\text{)}$$

A downward weight force on the shelf truss structure results from an upward acceleration equal to the acceleration of gravity. The X, Y and Z components of the acceleration of gravity are defined using the 'acel' command.

Add the following two data lines to the Tutorial 1A text file to include loading due to weight.

```
mp, dens, 1, 0.7331e-3          ! Material Property density
acel, 0, 386., 0                ! X, Y, Z components of gravity.
```

If the problem is being formulated by **interactive input**, the following selections and data inputs should be used.

When specifying the material properties, enter the mass density as well as the elastic modulus and Poisson's ratio. Double click on Density and enter its value.

Figure 9-1 Mass density input.

To enter the acceleration of gravity,

Main Menu > Preprocessor > Loads > Define Loads > Apply > Structural > Inertia > Gravity > Global Enter Y-comp **386.** > **OK**.

Figure 9-2 Acceleration of gravity input.

9-3 MULTIPLE LOAD CASES

Often we want to know the response of a system to more than one load condition. In the shelf truss problem for example, we might need to analyze the behavior under a side loading condition together with the downward load. Or the downward load might be considered by itself as one case, and the combination of downward and side loads as a second case. The support movement condition could then be added as a third case. There is no need to reformulate the problem three times to consider these combinations. The basic structural model does not change in any way, just the loadings.

ANSYS allows multiple load cases to be considered through the use of multiple load steps, a different step for each case. During preprocessing, each load case is defined and then written to a file to be used during the solution. In the solution phase this file is read and all load cases treated, not just the 'Current Load Step'. And finally in postprocessing, each load case (step) is view independently.

For Tutorial 1A with **fx = 0., fy = –300 lbf** at node 2 as **case one** and **fx = 100, fy = 0** at node 2 as **case two**, the input text file would be:

```
f, 2, fx, 0.
f, 2, fy, -300.
lswrite                  ! write load step to file

f, 2, fx, 100.
f, 2, fy, 0.
lswrite

/solu
antype,static

lssolve,1,2              ! Initiates solution for load step files 1 and 2
finish
```

The **interactive** commands for considering **multiple load cases** are: In the Preprocessor, use **Loads > Define Loads > Apply** to define the first load case as described earlier then select

Main Menu > Preprocessor > Loads > Load Step Opts > Write LS File (Give the load case a number) **> OK**

Figure 9-3 Write Load Step File.

Define the next load set (be sure to delete any loading not needed for the second set) and repeat the above.

Then read these load set files during the solution step.

Main Menu > Solution > Solve > From LS Files . . . (enter starting, ending, and increment) **> OK**

Figure 9-4 Solve load step files.

To evaluate the computed results,

Main Menu > GeneralPostproc > Read Results > First Set > Plot Results etc.

Then

Main Menu > GeneralPostproc > Read Results > Next Set > Plot Results etc.

Continue reading calculated results data sets, plotting, listing, etc until you have all of the results desired from the analysis.

9-4 ANSYS MATERIALS DATABASE

We have entered the materials data for all of the examples thus far, but ANSYS also provides a database of commonly used materials. (Access details depend on your local installation.)

Main Menu > Preprocessor > Material Props > Material Library > Select Units from **SI, CGS, BFT, BIN,** or **USER > OK.**

Main Menu > Preprocessor > Material Props > Material Library > Import Library Enter file names or browse (On Windows systems Program Files\Ansys Inc\V110\ANSYS\matlib) to find a data file in the ANSYS Matlib directory. Specify the material number **MAT** (1, 2, 3, etc.) for your model > **OK.**

The data file is displayed on the screen and is incorporated in your model database.

Data for **304 steel** in British system inch units (BIN) for example, is shown below.

```
LIST MATERIALS        1 TO        1 BY        1
  PROPERTY= ALL

 PROPERTY TABLE EX    MAT=        1  NUM. POINTS= 1
    TEMPERATURE       DATA    TEMPERATURE       DATA    TEMPERATURE       DATA
      0.0000      0.27993E+08

 PROPERTY TABLE NUXY  MAT=        1  NUM. POINTS= 1
    TEMPERATURE       DATA    TEMPERATURE       DATA    TEMPERATURE       DATA
      0.0000      0.29000

 PROPERTY TABLE ALPX  MAT=        1  NUM. POINTS= 1
    TEMPERATURE       DATA    TEMPERATURE       DATA    TEMPERATURE       DATA
      0.0000      0.98889E-05

 PROPERTY TABLE DENS  MAT=        1  NUM. POINTS= 1
    TEMPERATURE       DATA    TEMPERATURE       DATA    TEMPERATURE       DATA
      0.0000      0.75148E-03

 PROPERTY TABLE KXX   MAT=        1  NUM. POINTS= 1
    TEMPERATURE       DATA    TEMPERATURE       DATA    TEMPERATURE       DATA
      0.0000      0.21822E-03

 PROPERTY TABLE C     MAT=        1  NUM. POINTS= 1
    TEMPERATURE       DATA    TEMPERATURE       DATA    TEMPERATURE       DATA
      0.0000      46.286

 LIST DATA TABLE  ALL   FOR MATERIAL       1
```

9-5 ANSYS HELP

A wealth of on-line information is provided with the ANSYS software. Select **Help > Help Topics > Contents** from the Utility menu and the following information screen is displayed.

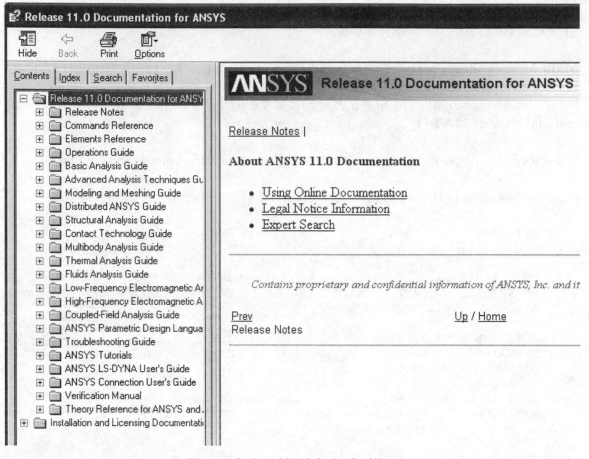

Figure 9-5 ANSYS help facility.

The contents shown include structural analysis and thermal analysis guides as well as an extensive set of verification problems and their data files that are labeled VMXX; XX is the verification problem number. A search of the references can also be performed using keyword search methods.

9-6 CONSTRAINTS

Often one wants to add constraints to the model in order to enforce certain conditions not inherent in the modeling discussed previously. One of these is the introduction of a **release** or **hinge** where two elements join, particularly useful for beam modeling.

Another involves modeling of **rigid** objects, which are not always properly represented by using a very, very stiff element because that can sometimes produce undesirable numerical effects.

Look for information on '**coupled sets**' in the documentation for more help with constraints.

9-7 NATURAL FREQUENCIES

The global stiffness and global mass matrices for a structure can be used to find the natural frequencies of vibration of the model. The mass matrix will be available if the **mass density** is supplied along with the other material properties (be sure you get the units right). ANSYS has a number of solution methods available to compute natural frequencies and modes of vibration. The solver that is selected depends upon the size of the problem under consideration and the number of frequencies desired as well as other factors.

Natural frequency calculation in ANSYS is called **MODAL ANALYSIS**; to extract the natural frequencies using the default method, use the steps outlined below.

After the model has been built: geometry, elements, materials, boundary conditions. (Loads, other than prestress loads, are not used in natural frequency analysis.)

Main Menu > Solution > Analysis Type > New Analysis > Modal > OK

Analysis Options > Block Lanczos

    No. of Modes to Extract (Enter number of frequencies you want to find.)

    Expand mode shapes > yes

    NMODE No. modes to expand (Enter number of mode shapes you want to find.)

    OK

    FREQB 0

    FREQE 0   Accept the defaults

Normalize modes **To Mass Matrix** (Gives orthonormal modes.) **> OK**

Calculate the natural frequencies.

Main Menu > Solution > Solve > Current LS > OK

Evaluate the results.

Main Menu > General Postprocessor > Results Summary (Displays the calculated frequencies in Hz.)

Observe the computed mode shapes.

Main Menu > General Postprocessor > Read Results > First Set

Main Menu > General Postprocessor > Plot Results > Deformed Shape > Def. + Undef.

The **first mode** of vibration is shown.

It is also very helpful use **PlotCtrls > Animate** to visualize the motion. The 'raise hidden' button near the top of the screen can be used to display the **Animation Controller** window to manipulate the display.

Use **List Results > Nodal Solution > DOF solution > All DOFs** to list the mode shape.

For the next mode **Read Results > Next Set**

Plot Results > Deformed Shape > Def. + Undef. , continue for all modes of interest.

Try this using the L-shaped beam of Lesson 5. Add the mass density to the file and compute the first two modes. Verify that mode 1 is a bending mode, while mode 2 is a torsion type mode.

Note that the computed frequencies are given in cycles/second (Hz). Modes can be normalized with the largest displacement value set to 1.0 or normalized on the mass matrix so that the generalized mass terms are all 1.0 (orthonormal modes).

9-8 ANSYS Files

A number of permanent and temporary files are used by ANSYS during the solution of a typical problem. These have the form *.*ext* where * is the Jobname and *ext* is an extension which is used to identify the data stored in the file. If ANSYS starts with a blank Jobname, the default name is set to '**file**'.

Some files are text (ASCII) files and some are binary files. Among the most important are the following:

*.db - A binary file that stores the job database. It can contain model data (geometry, materials, elements, etc.), model data plus solution results, or model, solution and postprocessing data. The exact contents depend upon how the db file is saved. The **File > Save as Jobname.db** (or **Save as**) command will save the model and solution results if the solution has been performed. The **QUIT (Exit) > Save . . .** provides options to save part, all or none of the data currently in memory.

*.rst - The binary file that contains the results of a **structural** analysis and is created when the solution step is performed.

*.rth - The binary results file for a **thermal** analysis.

*.log - A text file that contains all the command instructions from a session with ANSYS. It can be used to recreate a session by using the **Read Input from** menu choice to read commands contained in the log file. New sessions append to the existing log file when ANSYS starts, so using *.log as input requires that you cut and paste to select the session in question or plan ahead and delete *.log before starting a session whose commands you want to preserve for later use. The log file provides a way to convert an interactive session into a text file definition of a specific analysis. CDWRITE is another way of doing this but uses the db file.

*.err - A text file containing error and warning messages written during an analysis.

*.dbb - Binary file which is a copy of the db file.

To retrieve a model, all that is needed is the db file. The db file will contain model, model and solution, or model, solution, and postprocessing data depending upon how it was saved.

9-9 SUMMARY

The number of possible ANSYS modeling and solution options is extremely large, and this lesson has presented a few that may be of interest.

NOTES:

Index

NOTES:

NOTES:

NOTES:

NOTES:

NOTES:

NOTES: